GALINA K[...]

RUNES:

THEORY & PRACTICE

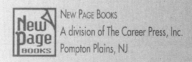
NEW PAGE BOOKS
A division of The Career Press, Inc.
Pompton Plains, NJ

RUNES: THEORY & PRACTICE
EDITED BY KIRSTEN DALLEY
TYPESET BY EILEEN MUNSON
Cover design by *The* Book Designers
Printed in the U.S.A.

To order this title, please call toll-free 1-800-CAREER-1 (NJ and Canada: 201-848-0310) to order using VISA or MasterCard, or for further information on books from Career Press.

The Career Press, Inc., 220 West Parkway, Unit 12
Pompton Plains, NJ 07444
www.careerpress.com
www.newpagebooks.com

Library of Congress Cataloging-in-Publication Data

Krasskova, Galina, 1972-
    Runes : theory & practice / by Galina Krasskova.
        p. cm.
    Includes bibliographical references and index.
    ISBN 978-1-60163-085-8
        1. Fortune-telling by runes. 2. Runes. I. Title.

BF1891.R85K73 2010
133.3'3--dc22

                                                           2009036391

Dedication — — — — — — — — — — — —

To my adopted mother,
who does not work the runes
and hates magic with a passion,
but who listened to early versions of this book
with the patience of a saint.
Ich habe dich unendlich gern auf Zeit und Ewigkeit, Mutti.
Thank you so much for everything.

And to those who taught me, with gratitude.

Acknowledgments — — — — — — — —

Many thanks to Raven Kaldera for allowing me to quote from his work on the Futhorc runes, and to Elizabeth Vongvisith for providing me with 32 beautiful modern-day rune poems.

To my friends and colleagues, who patiently tolerated my increasingly cranky mood as my deadline approached.

And, finally, to my editors at New Page books, most especially Michael Pye and Kirsten Dalley. It's been a pleasure working with you once more. Thank you for all your hard work!

*C*ontents

Introduction

This is not an introductory book on runes, though it does cover the basic precepts. There are many good introductory books on rune-work available. I have noted several worthy texts in the Bibliography and Suggested Reading sections, and I encourage my readers to seek them out. Nor is this a historical overview of the runes, even though I am an academic. Although I believe that a clear understanding of the historical context in which the runes evolved is important, that is not the purpose of this book. Scholars debate whether or not the runes were ever used magically. As an Odin's woman, mystic, and rune worker speaking specifically to the Northern Tradition religious community, I know they were. I cannot write about runes in this particular context as an academic. So what, then, is the purpose of this book?

This is the book that I wish I had had access to when I was first starting out more than two decades ago. This is the book that I wish I could have given my first students when they came to me so long ago wishing to learn the runes. This book, which I believe is the first of its kind, is drawn from reams of notes that I developed over time and used to introduce students and apprentices to the runes. It offers a detailed description of what I believe, based on years of experience, to be the nature and lessons of each rune, and a systematic methodology for learning to access them.

Most importantly of all, it teaches the would-be rune-worker to approach the runes as living spirits and to develop a relationship with them as sentient, independent spirit allies. It presents a protocol of practice which, if diligently followed, will enable the saavy rune student to work as painlessly as possible in this art, avoiding many common pitfalls. With the exception of a brief section in Raven Kaldera's *Northern Tradition Shamanism* series (available through Asphodel Press), I know of no other book on runes that discusses their nature as living beings and what that means for the rune worker. This book fills that gap.

I begin this book with an exegesis on the story of Odin's winning of the runes by sacrifice. Drawing on comparative mythologies throughout Northern Europe as well as developing practices within contemporary Heathenry, I will explore the ideas of ordeal, sacrifice, pain, agency, and power as they relate to the runes. Subsequent chapters look at the theory and practice of magic, the art of galdr, the craft of divination, and potential ethical problems inherent in this type of work. Chapter 3 explores the individual runes one by one, including both the Elder Futhark and the younger Anglo-Saxon Futhorc. Much of this chapter is drawn directly from my personal gnosis as a rune magician and diviner. Finally, a thorough list of resources is provided.

This book presupposes a reasonable knowledge of Norse cosmology and a basic knowledge of energy-working skills (that is, magic). It also presupposes a desire to interact on some authentic level with the Norse Gods and Goddesses. The study of runes can be difficult and challenging but it can also be immensely rewarding. I encourage each of my readers to use this book as a stepping stone toward developing their own unique and individual relationship with the runes. Ultimately, to quote an Estonian proverb, "the work will teach you how to do it." Good luck.

1 Odin:
The First Rune-Master

O din is the high God in the Northern Tradition. In both the surviving sources and in modern Heathenry, He is referred to variously as the All-Father, Victory Father, Hanging God, Old Man, or Old One-Eye.[1] One of the defining aspects of His nature, as attested to in the Norse myths, is His insatiable thirst for knowledge and wisdom. This thirst for knowledge led Odin to seek out the runes, and He did so by sacrificing Himself on the Norse World-Tree: Yggdrasil. Modern Northern Tradition Shamans such as Raven Kaldera refer to Odin as the God of the Ordeal. The Ordeal Path as practiced by modern Northern Tradition Shamans (and others) involves the "intentional and careful use of pain in order to put the body into an altered state."[2] One could say that the use of pain in such a fashion lies at the heart of Odin's sacrifice to win the runes.[3]

The story of Odin's primary ordeal is told in the Havamal, one of the lays of the *Poetic Edda*. The reader is told that in search of wisdom, Odin hung Himself for nine days and nights on Yggdrasil, the World-Tree. Although Odin is usually viewed as a God of kingship, He also holds a place within the Northern Tradition as a God of shamans. The idea of a great cosmic tree that supports the universe and which can be utilized by shamans in spirit-travel is common to many northern European cultures, most notably the Yakut and Buryat.[4] The Tree shows up again in Jewish Cabbala in the guise of the Tree of Life, and has one of its earliest manifestations in Sumerian stories of the Goddess Inanna. It is by traversing the World-Tree that Odin is able to move from His role as sacred king to that of Shaman. The key to this transition from temporal to liminal power was His sacrifice by hanging.

During this ordeal, He starved Himself and stabbed Himself with His own spear, shedding His own blood. Eventually He died. It is through His death and rebirth that He gained access to the runes, the keys to the secrets of the universe:

> I ween that I hung on the windy tree,
>
> Hung there for nights full nine;
>
> With the spear I was wounded, and offered I was
>
> To Othin, myself to myself,
>
> On the tree that none may ever know
>
> What root beneath it runs.[5]

Odin then recited the charms that He learned, and set down the formula for making appropriate sacrifices by providing a list of ritual acts including divination, blood offering, petitioning the Gods and making actual sacrifice.[6] Although many modern Heathens look at this passage as esoteric lore solely concerned with the reading of runes for divination, many scholars, most notably, the German historian Rudolf Simek, believe it to be a complex list of ritual actions, one that specifically references sacrifice.[7] Odin's sacrifice permeates modern Heathen consciousness. It is one of the defining moments in the religion's mythos.

The use of pain as a spiritual tool is quite controversial in modern Heathenry. It is, however, part and parcel of

Odin's story. In his book *Dark Moon Rising*, Raven Kaldera notes that "cultures all over the world have explored ways to use the power of pain as a spiritual tool."[8] He references the Lakota sun dance and the Hindu Kavadi, and notes that "the technique of applied pain is probably older than that of psychoactive substances,"[9] yet another Shamanic practice with which Odin is associated. Although Northern Tradition Shamanic practices are somewhat outside the scope of this book, the idea of sacrifice (whatever that might mean to the individual) to gain wisdom is deeply entrenched in the core cosmological ethos of northern religions. This has evolved within a small subsection of the modern Northern Tradition into the practice of ordeal work.

Ordeal work refers to a body of practices used to bring about a deep catharsis for purposes such as self-growth, religious sacrifice, or a rite of passage. These practices quite often involve physical pain, and are usually done in a spiritual or at least a carefully crafted context. Practitioners maintain that when utilized in a controlled manner, ordeal practices have the power to heal, transform, and render the practitioner receptive to their Gods.[10]

The use of pain-based rites for spiritual reasons had many corollaries in the ancient world. Priests of the Goddess Cybele, for example, would slash their bodies with knives, giving their own blood in offering. At its most extreme manifestation, devotees would castrate themselves in a similar manner at the conclusion of rituals filled with ecstatic dancing.[11] During specific religious festivals, Hindu devotees may perform *Kavadi*—piercing the body with hooks or spikes, ideally to provoke spirit possession.[12] Lest this be mistaken for an Eastern phenomenon, it is worth noting that numerous Native American tribes still perform the sun dance, a sacrificial dance in which dancers have hooks inserted into their flesh, which are then secured to a central tree or post (again, we see the imagery of the tree recurring as a central theme). They then dance until the hooks tear free of their flesh.[13] We also have the example of the Spanish Christian *flagellantes* who still perform rites of flagellation in honor of Christ. By engaging in such practices, practitioners of the ordeal position themselves as living sacrifices to their Gods. It is not coincidental that the majority of ordeal workers within the Northern Tradition are devotees of Odin. Although Odin is not just a God of the ordeal (far from it), ordeal work is one of the many things for which He is known.[14] He is a God of sacrifice, most especially the sacrifice of the self. Historian E. Turville-Petre points out that

> the sacrifice of Odin to himself may...be seen as the highest conceivable form of sacrifice, in fact so high that, like many a religious mystery, it surpasses our comprehension. It is the sacrifice, not of king to god, but of god to god of such a kind as is related in Scripture of the sacrifice of Christ.[15]

Nor was this similarity with the sacrifice of Christ lost on early converts to Christianity. One of the earliest known Anglo-Saxon Christian poems, *The Dream of the Rood*, dating from the 7th century CE, uses imagery suited to both Christ and Odin. Pagan themes abound:

> The young hero stripped himself—he, God Almighty—
> strong and stout-minded. He mounted high gallows,
> bold before many, when he would loose mankind.
> I shook when that Man clasped me. I dared, still, not bow to earth,
> fall to earth's fields, but had to stand fast.
> Rood was I reared. I lifted a mighty King,
> Lord of the heavens, dared not to bend.

With dark nails they drove me through: on me
those sores are seen,
open malice-wounds. I dared not scathe
anyone.
They mocked us both, we two together. All
wet with blood I was,
poured out from that Man's side, after ghost
he gave up.
Much have I born on that hill
of fierce fate. I saw the God of hosts
harshly stretched out.[16]

Here the reader is presented with the image of a warrior-Christ, courageously sacrificing Himself. The poem is told from the perspective of the tree itself, and the reference to the tree as a gallows willingly mounted would immediately conjure the image of Odin to the Pagan mind. One of his by-names is, after all, the "Gallows God," (Yggdrasil being a type of gallows). Christ like Odin is also viewed as a mighty king, and both shared the attribution of "Lord of Hosts."[17]

In short, both Odin and Christ hung and died. Both were pierced by a spear. Both rose again into new life. Both were seen as sacral kings. The difference between Them lies in the reasons behind Their respective sacrifices: Christ, according to common Christian interpretation, hung to free humanity of its sins—in other words, as a scapegoat; Odin hung for Himself alone, to deepen his wisdom and expand his power to order the world. He hung to gain sovereignty as a king, not just over the temporal world but over the spirit world, as well. The only way to gain and master the wisdom of the dead was to die. Folklorist James Frazer points out that kings were often revered not merely as rulers but also as priests, intercessors between the human world and the Gods. This stemmed in part from the ritual deification of the king as a divine figure himself.[18] In Odin, the function of king is united with the

RUNES: THEORY & PRACTICE

function of priest, magician, and Shaman. That union occurs through purposefully sought-after ordeals, and each ordeal involves some form of sacrifice.

Hanging on Yggdrasil was not the only sacrifice that Odin made in the surviving mythos. In addition to His sacrifice on the World-Tree, He also hung suspended between two fires in the *Grimnismal* and plucked out an eye in payment for a single drink from the Well of Memory and Wisdom. This willing loss of an eye is particularly interesting. Odin is never depicted in any known image or account with both eyes intact. The resulting iconography of the one-eyed God is one of the defining symbols within Norse cosmology. Unlike the blind seer, Tiresias, of Greek mythos, Odin was not blinded as a result of experienced wisdom or by a punitive Deity; rather, He chose to partially blind himself in order to gain wisdom. His blinding, then, was an act of power.[19]

The submission to pain as an act of personal empowerment raises many questions not only about the nature of pain but also about the nature of personal agency. A clear distinction must be drawn between pain as a *cause* of action and pain as a *kind* of action.[20] It is this latter manifestation of pain that is illustrated in Odin's story. Here, pain is used not as an externally repressive measure, but as an expression of personal sovereignty.[21] Anthropologist Talal Asad notes that "when we say that someone is suffering, we commonly suppose that he or she is not an agent. To suffer…is, so we usually think, to be in a passive state—to be an object, not a subject."[22] In Odin, however, the reader is presented with the image of a suffering body engaged in an act of power, or, as modern ordeal workers might phrase it, "hunting for power."[23] In this context, pain loses its emotional charge and becomes a consciously applied tool in a greater process of development. Pain becomes something more than a private experience or an experience of utter loss of control. It becomes an act of power.[24]

Not only pain, but blindness and the paradox of sacrificing sight in order to gain vision, permeates Odin's mythos. Several of his *heiti*, or by-names, refer to His vision: *Blindr* ("blind one"), *Gestumblindi* ("the blind guest"), *Tviblindi* ("doubly blind"). According to Indo-European historian Kris Kershaw, depending on the context in which the symbology of the blind God is used in the poetic sources, it designates Odin not only as one who is Himself blind, but also as one who has the power to strike others blind (as a battle tactic, or perhaps a blindness of ecstasy or desire—two qualities also associated strongly with this God).[25] We also have *Gunnblindi* ("he who strikes others blind in battle"), *Herblindi* ("he who strikes armies with blindness"), *Bileygr* ("weak-eyed"), and *Bálegyr* ("flaming eye").[26] If the eyes are the windows into the soul, as the saying goes, in sacrificing one eye, Odin sacrificed part of His soul in exchange for wisdom, which hearkens back to the Eddic proverb that a gift demands an equal gift in return.

Odin is one of several mutilated or self-mutilating Gods in Northern European mythology. In Irish mythology, for instance, King Nuada of the Tuatha de Danaan lost an arm in battle and later replaced it with a functioning silver replica. In the Norse pantheon, the God Tyr sacrifices a hand. There is the blind God, Hodr, but almost no information about His function has survived. Although the particulars of Hodr's blindness are unknown, in the cases of both Nuada and Tyr, their respective sacrifices occurred as a necessary exchange for the protection and security of their people: Nuada lost his arm in battle, ending a great war that was destroying his people, and Tyr sacrificed his hand to Fenris, the wolf of chaos and destruction, in order to bind the animal and thus prevent it from its fated goal of bringing destruction to the Gods. It is a small step from the idea of physical mutilation as sacrifice to the idea of human sacrifice.[27]

In *Germania*, the Roman historian Tacitus makes note of human sacrifice to Odin, and apparently this was done in a very specific manner: usually by hanging the victim while piercing his side with a spear. One of the most well-known examples of a sacrifice of this kind to Odin occurs in Gautrek's Saga, a 13th-century retelling of the story of the Odinic hero, Starkadr. It includes a tale of sacrifice centering on Starkadr's King, Vikarr. While sailing, King Vikarr and his crew (which included his friend, blood brother, and one of Odin's chosen heroes, the aforementioned Starkadr) experienced horrible storm winds. They cast runes to determine how to calm the storm, and as the storm winds abated, it was revealed through divination that Odin demanded a sacrifice. Turville-Petre notes that Odin was usually placated by royal victims, perhaps a nod to his role as sacred king.[28] The majority of recorded victims in the surviving skaldic narratives were kings or princes, usually warriors. The men drew lots to determine who should be sacrificed, and, predictably, it turned out to be the king himself. (By drawing lots, the choice was automatically put into the hands of Odin and the Fates). Therefore the men decided to hold a symbolic sacrifice rather than actually kill their King. The men fastened a cord made of calf gut loosely around Vikarr's neck, tying the other end to a thin branch. Neither would bear a man's weight. Starkadr then struck the King with a slender reed, uttering the words, "Now I give thee to Odin." At that moment, the reed became a spear and the cord a rope noose and the King was sacrificed.[29]

The sacrifice of a king is well known throughout folklore. Folklorist James Frazer notes that kings were often sacrificed as old age or infirmity took hold. In other cases, the king might be sacrificed at the end of a fixed period of time. There is a story, for instance, linking Odin with this latter type of sacrifice. Frazer writes of King Aun of Sweden, who received the gift that he would be allowed to live and reign as long as he continued to sacrifice one of his sons every nine years. This continued for nine consecutive sacrifices until the king was so feeble and incompetent that his own people prevented the

10th sacrifice.[30] There is no indication in the story of Vikarr that the king was anything less than capable. Rather, it seems that Odin as God of warriors might instead choose the best and most virile of kings to join Him in Valhalla, the hall the valorous were believed to go to after death.

It is clear from these examples that Odin is a fierce and complex figure within Norse cosmology. While I cannot speak for every devotee of Odin, I have found in nearly two decades of serving, honoring, and, most of all, loving Him, that He is 10,000 times more demanding of Himself than He is of His followers. Those who seek to work with the runes with any level of useful skill should meditate long and hard on the sacrifices Odin made and the trials He undertook in order to win the right to use them. Sooner or later, rune-workers, too, may be asked to pay a price. What that price is will vary from person to person, but in the world of the runes, as within the greater macrocosm of the Northern Tradition, there are no free rides. That, above all, is one of Odin's most important lessons. It is one to keep in mind as one begins exploring the runes.

2 The Runes as Spirit Allies

Working with runes takes immeasurable skill and endurance. Odin, after all, had to die for them, hanging as He did on the World-Tree for nine nights of agony. Runes are not easily won, nor are they easily wielded. They can be ruthless and brutal teachers. For all those Northern Traditionists who decry folks such as Ralph Blum dabbling in runic mysteries, the runes themselves are quite capable of keeping the unworthy and untested from making any useful headway. Working with them is almost like engaging in a cosmic tug-of-war with the will and the power they wield. Or sometimes it can be like playing with razor blades. The majority of them tend to be rather pitiless, at least until they have tested the rune-worker (and, many times, not even after that). There is nothing human about the runes and that is the most important thing to remember. The only humanity they hold is the blood that has been given them by countless *vitki* (rune-workers and magicians).

Runes are far more than a simple method of divination or even a system of magic. At their core, they are living keys to accessing and working the Wyrd, but even this function only barely touches on their true nature. The runes are alive. It's not enough to simply cast them; at the higher levels, one must realize that they have an instinct and intellect all their own, and a very potent will. They can be powerful allies or adamantly vicious enemies, but they are anything but static and inert sigils. This is something that most people who work with runes don't seem to realize. They're sentient. They are allies, in the traditional spirit-sense.

There are levels of skill in working with the runes and there is no shame at all in being a beginner or in choosing to restrict one's interaction to pure divination. Essentially, runes will open up only so much and no further to the novice; one must keep coming back again and again to explore them. Only when the relationship is solid and well-developed will the individual runes begin to allow the vitki or diviner a little more access. This is obviously a life-long endeavor. Runes are most popular today as a divination tool, and they can be amazingly effective in this capacity. However, the same caveat applies: They won't allow themselves to be read until they've begun testing the reader in some way. I've heard experienced tarot readers complain about how difficult it is to read with the runes. They are unable to figure out why they could read so well with tarot but hardly at all with the runes, even after much study. I myself have had the runes outright refuse to read specific querents, or demand an offering before they'd agree to reveal Wyrd.

Furthermore, the runes are patently uninterested in seeking out humanity. When they unite with the vitki in whatever way they are being called, be it for magic, galdr, meditation, or divination, the rune-worker is touching, however briefly, a world that existed before the coming of the Gods. They are touching spirits that thrived when the worlds collided at the beginning of time. There is something primordial and ancient yet forever youthful about certain of the runes. It is as if all time and all experience is bound up in them. As infrequently as they seek out humanity, part of their being is still bound up in the flow and fabric of time, and human experience is part of that.

The runes are organic. There is a reason Odin was on the Tree when He snatched them up. There's a reason they are fed blood. So the language of the runes is also organic. In allowing a rune-worker to access their power, it isn't a question of the runes coldly shutting someone out for lack of skill; rather, it is their revealing the organic meaning of their interpretation and nature. The rune-worker must learn their language. Consider the justice rune, Tiewaz, for example: This rune does not conform to whatever a vitki's idea of justice is. The rune itself is fed with its own notion or ideas of justice. The rune will most probably not work for a vitki until that person understands the rune's own conception of justice. In a way, this is a fail-safe mechanism to prevent the novice from swimming in waters he or she may not be ready for. Runes, whether they contact or are contacted by us, try to make sure that we understand their nature and how far they can manipulate that nature while still being true to themselves.

So, early on, a rune-master must learn to neither ignore what the rune is saying (that is, the language of the rune) nor become overly manipulated by it. When you're chanting the rune, even if you are aiming for a specific goal, you cannot ignore where the rune is trying to take you. They work within the confines of their own natures. At the same time, you can, to an extent, get the rune to understand what you're trying to accomplish and point it in the right direction. Runes work by understanding and partnership, not by domination. A rune such as Thurisaz will be more likely to work for you if you approach it fully understanding and accepting all the capacities of that rune and what that means. If you do not feel you can harness or even project destructive energy, and thus feel that Thurisaz won't tap into those areas because they're not in your nature, you may encounter serious problems. The rules of good conversation can be very helpful when working with the runes. You neither cut off the other person too soon nor allow them to talk on endlessly. The give and take of good conversational dynamics is exactly the relationship that the vitki has with a given rune at the moment of perfect working. The runes cooperate more readily when you understand and accept their full potential, rather than trying to ignore certain aspects because you may not find those characteristics in your own nature.

For this reason, rune-workers may find it easier to work with certain runes than others. Commonality of nature and personality may lead to certain relationships becoming stronger than others at an earlier stage. For instance, I work quite comfortably and well with Ansuz, but I find Mannaz to be extremely difficult to access. Both I and the rune are willing but we haven't yet found a point of commonality upon which to build the relationship. I don't yet speak its language fluently enough. Sometimes, these things take time. And sometimes, though the runes will come when you call them, they may not open their energies to you for a very long time. Often, when I was first learning how to work with the runes, my initial galdr sessions would involve no magic at all, but rather, simple exploration of the rune itself.

The fluidity of galdr prepares one exceptionally well for rune-work. The voice becomes the perfect conduit for their power, even if all one is doing is tasting their essence and nature. Through galdr (which need not be particularly euphonic), the rune-worker can access points on the Wyrd-web that would otherwise be far out of reach. An excellent exercise is to spend several days with each rune, singing not only the rune name, but any images, sounds, smells, or feelings that come to mind while concentrating on and reaching out for the rune. Eventually, words will fall by the wayside and the voice will convey pure, raw power without the limitation or interference of words. Runes have rhythm and vibration and movement. This, too, is extremely important when one is getting to know them. Although Deity possession (a common practice in Afro-Caribbean religions) is gaining ground in certain denominations of the Northern Tradition, the runes do not possess people. However, their energies can flow through the vitki's body, and it can augment certain magical workings if the practitioner knows how to express that energy in chanting, singing, dancing, movement, and so on. Their language is not strictly verbal; as such, galdr is an expression of the rune itself. In listening to galdr, you're listening to the sound and vibrations of the threads of Wyrd, not the vibrations of your own vocal chords. This is why it can sound so dissonant. It's not important how it sounds to human ears, but how it reverberates on the Wyrd-web. It just takes time to develop the ability to hear that.

Anyone seeking to access the runes should have at least a basic understanding of Wyrd. Runes can follow the rune-master almost anywhere (and they do, because they assume that the rune-master understands Wyrd). It's not that they are amoral; rather, it's more that they trust the rune-master to understand the consequences of putting whatever it is he or she is casting into the web. They won't necessarily stop you once you've gained their trust. Some people when they work magic have the attitude that if the universe is allowing them to do it, it must mean that they have some sort of cosmic permission. Runes are not like this. Their attitude is more along the lines of "if you're foolish enough, or bold enough, or whatever enough, to cast this, then you will reap what you sow." The runes will do their job and sit back and watch the proverbial fireworks. Learn how to balance Wyrd and move within its strands and eddies before seeking out the runes. The initial stages of developing a working relationship with the runes can actually teach this to a great degree.

There's an advantage to the fact that runes are sentient. In rune-magic, the rune-master and the rune itself both absorb part of the responsibility. When casting, however, you must be very sure to accept the responsibility that is yours to accept and, equally as important, give what isn't yours to keep to the rune. The rune can hold more of that—a lot more—than you can. This is important when it comes to magical backlash. You may be able to endure the backlash for a botched casting in the amount that is rightfully yours, but if you inadvertently shoulder what belongs to the rune itself, you may well be crushed beneath the weight.

In divinatory readings, the fact that runes are sentient can also be a great boon. It's not just a matter of using your own gifts of precognition and discernment to read Wyrd and Fate; the runes can actually talk to you. It becomes a dance of reciprocity and conversation. Although it may seem strange to the average querent to be talking to his or her "tools," it makes for much more thorough readings.

At this point, I feel it's necessary to issue a caveat: At some point, all runes like to be fed blood. Certain ones demand it before lending their energies to task at hand, so be prepared for this. If you want to work with them well, they will likely want to feed on your blood. To this end, I suggest keeping a box of diabetic lancets and some alcohol swabs handy. These can be easily purchased in almost any drugstore and do not require a prescription. Use an alcohol swab on your finger and then prick it with the lancet. Put the resulting few drops of blood directly on the rune. I recommend going through them individually and "blooding" them at regular intervals. Once you begin working with them at any deep level, they will demand this.

Runes find the English language quite alien. This is important to know because when you start working with them, they will often give you very specific images, and few of these images are connected to 21st-century America. They also assign very different values to things such as money, death, and sex. They more readily communicate their ideas using the language and symbology of Norse cosmology. They cannot be forced to adhere to the parlance or values of American culture. They use whatever cultural construct that is closest to the language they speak.

Pain is also a tool that certain runes will use, for it opens the consciousness of the rune-worker in ways that friendlier tools, such as ecstasy and sexual pleasure, do not. Understand that human morality is not part and parcel of the nature of the runes. All one has to do is look at what Odin had to go through to initially access them to understand the perils and challenges of this work. They do not open readily to people who are overly concerned about maintaining socially acceptable appearances or the status quo. There is something about their domain that favors those who tend to extremes. Most of all, they favor the shift in consciousness that occurs when one fully commits to the work at hand.

The runes influence one another. It's impossible to fully understand a rune by itself. Ultimately, one must understand their place in the Futhark order, their relationships with each other, and their relationships with the Gods (who each tend to favor certain runes). Ansuz, for instance, is generally considered Odin's rune. Understanding why this is so can do much for increasing one's understanding of the rune itself. Understanding why Ansuz follows Thurisaz is equally enlightening and important. Just as the Wyrd-web is constructed of interlocking and layered threads, so the runes exist in a dynamic, interwoven, interrelated, shifting paradigm of energies. In this respect, they reflect the complexity of the web itself. It is impossible to separate the runes from Wyrd. They are living extensions and reflections of it.

Finally, when one seeks to understand and work with the runes, it's important to realize that, sooner or later, one will encounter Odin. This has the potential to take one's rune-work to an entirely new level of experience and intensity. Even in the early stages, Odin can certainly provide advice on the best way to approach the runes. This, of course, may attract His attention in ways the rune-worker might not be prepared for. It's best to understand that He is the ultimate Rune-Master and that, sooner or later, the road to every rune leads to Him.

Because the runes are living entities, it is important to establish an actively reciprocal relationship with them from the very beginning, just as if you were dealing with a recognized spirit or even a Deity. They are hungry and can be quite challenging. They need to be courted and sacrificed to in order to reveal themselves to the rune-worker, and this only occurs over a period of time—just like forming any relationship, with its attendant building of trust.

I recommend beginning your rune studies with the following offertory rite. It starts the relationship off on a positive note. It's very important to remember that the runes are sentient, with a will and agenda of their own, but they are not human. They will make their wishes and requirements known. The following ritual involves introducing yourself, making specific offerings, and putting your desire and vow to study directly into the web of Wyrd. It also involves making offerings to Odin as Galdra-Father and Rune-Master. He's the best guide one can have through the runes, *but* (and this is a big but) one of His major lessons is that nothing comes without its price and, sooner or later, that will figure into your own work with the runes.

Ritual of Your Offering to the Runes

Begin by setting up an altar to the runes. If possible, it should include an image of Odin (or at least things that are symbolic of Him) as well as symbols of the Nornir: Urd (that which was), Verdande (that which is becoming), and Skuld (obligation, causality, and consequences). Your runes should be set up in a circle around an offering bowl. You will also need a diabetic lancet with which to draw blood. Consecrate the space in whatever manner you find appropriate. Have a representation of fire on one side of the runes and a bowl of cold water or ice on the other (representing the two proto-worlds, Muspellheim and Niflheim, from which all life began). Then, make a paste of the following ingredients, using roughly equal amounts of each:

- Red ochre
- High quality cacao
- Henna powder
- Alder sap
- Tobacco
- Dragon's blood powder
- Honey
- Your own blood (only a few drops)
- High quality ground coffee
- Ground amber
- Any powdered or ground herbs you feel are appropriate

(When I did this, I chose a specific herb for each of the runes and added it to the mixture. Meditating on a particular rune to discover which herb it wanted was a powerful exercise in and of itself.) Then, grind everything together in a mortar and pestle and set this paste in a bowl on the altar. Many of the original substances you're adding are traditional blood substitutes. Red ochre, the blood of Midgard (the earth), can forge a particularly strong connection to the most primal of Ancestors. Additionally there should be a circle of tea lights around the runes (one for each rune) and six large candles.

I. Offering to the Ancestors

Say:

> "May my honored dead open my eyes,
> uncloud my vision, unloose my tongue and

clear my ears, that I may see what is woven
in the threads to see and hear the wisdom
whispered there. I ask that you guide me in
this work. I offer this, to you my honored
dead."

(Everyone's Ancestors like different things so at this
point name whatever it is you're offering to them.
Bread and beer are probably the most common
offerings. Or, you can name individual Ancestors. Feel
free to expand upon the prayer or write your own.)

Light one of the large candles.

II. Offering and Prayer to Odin

Pour a large glass or chalice of aquavit or some other
sufficiently strong liquor (such as good port, whiskey, or
red wine) into a glass and add a few drops of your blood.
(Note that it's probably best not to offer blood to Odin
unless you belong to Him.) Offer this to Odin with the
words:

Master of Runes, I come before You drawn
by their power.

I seek knowledge. I seek wisdom and
understanding.

Mighty Odin, Lord of Asgard, Hanging God,
Galdra-Father

I beg You to aid me on this quest.

May I learn rightly to read what is writ in the
web.

May I hear clearly the whisperings of the
runes

and bear their wisdom back to Midgard with
surety, humility, and clarity of purpose.

Teach me, Master of power, the proper sacrifices to make: how to read, how to write, how to offer, how to sacrifice that the runes might share their mysteries with me as well.

Ruthless One, You who murdered Yourself for their secrets

I ask Your guidance as I begin my own work with these sigils You so boldly won

by the strength and terror of that first offering, hanging nine nights on the body of the most terrible of Trees.

May I be bold.

May I be steadfast in this work.

Please teach me, Odin and guide my learning.

I make this offering to You.

Set out the alcohol and light one of the large candles. Again, you may not want to give the blood if you don't belong to Odin, .but see what your own Patron or Matron Deity says about it and go from there.

III. Offering to Your Patron/ess

Because everyone has had a different Deity claiming them, I haven't written a specific prayer here. Recite a similar prayer to the Offering to the Ancestors to your Patron/ Patroness/Divine Owner asking for aid and insight. Make an appropriate offering and light one of the large candles.

IV. Offering to the Nornir

Light one of the large candles and a stick of incense for each of the following prayers:

"I honor Urd, who spins the web, memory's mother, by the mouth of the Well. May I have

Your blessings on this endeavor."

"I honor Verdande, She who becomes,
Midgard's measurer who lays the threads. My
I have Your blessings on this endeavor."

"I honor Skuld, who orders the layers,
cutter of threads, determining price and
consequence clearly earned. May I have Your
blessings on this endeavor."

"May the smoke of this incense carry my
prayers to the Tree and may my work with the
runes receive the Sisters' blessings."

*If you wish to offer more to the Nornir it's not be a bad
idea. A glass of alcohol for each would be welcomed.*

V. Setting of Your Contract in Wyrd

*Prick your finger and offer a few drops of blood into the
flame representing Muspellheim, and a few drops into the
bowl of ice or water representing Niflheim, saying:*

"I honor Wyrd, the weaving of Fate and all the
consequence it brings. May I learn rightly, use justly
and never dishonor the teachings of the Tree. Let
this offering here speak to the worlds of this willingly
accepted obligation. May it be so."

(Note: Make sure you dispose of the water or ice responsibly. I
suggest flushing it down the toilet. It is important when working
with blood to ensure that no one else comes into contact with
your bodily fluids, if only for hygiene's sake. To this end, do
not reuse or share lancets or dispose of them sloppily. I keep
a "sharps" container, easily available at most pharmacies, on
hand in my house for the lancets. When it is full I dispose of it
at my doctor's office. Please be responsible. Used lancets are
biohazards.)

VI. Honoring the Runes

Progressing through the Elder Futhark, dab the paste on each rune and light a tea light in offering to that rune, saying as you go:

"Hail to Fehu, fire of life.
   Please accept this offering.

Hail to Uruz, primal power.
   Please accept this offering.

Hail to Thurisaz, hungry destroyer.
   Please accept this offering.

Hail to Ansuz, breath of Odin.
   Please accept this offering.

Hail to Raido, unstoppable momentum.
   Please accept this offering.

Hail to Kenaz, torch of learning.
   Please accept this offering.

Hail to Gebo, bliss and pain.
   Please accept this offering.

Hail to Wunjo, ecstatic blessings.
   Please accept this offering.

Hail to Hagalaz, ancestral doorway.
   Please accept this offering.

Hail to Nauthiz, constraint and need.
   Please accept this offering.

Hail to Isa, ice and power.
   Please accept this offering.

Hail to Jera, cycles and secrets.
   Please accept this offering.

Hail to Eihwaz, sacrificial tree.
   Please accept this offering.

Hail to Perthro, bottomless well.
   Please accept this offering.

Hail to Algiz, Valkyries' bower.
  Please accept this offering.

Hail to Sowelo, Sunna's shower.
  Please accept this offering.

Hail to Tiewaz, warrior's might.
  Please accept this offering.

Hail to Berkana, hard-won growth.
  Please accept this offering.

Hail to Ehwaz, spirit-horse.
  Please accept this offering.

Hail to Mannaz, dynamic union.
  Please accept this offering.

Hail to Laguz, water's wisdom.
  Please accept this offering.

Hail to Inguz, sacrificial blessing.
  Please accept this offering.

Hail to Dagaz, transformation.
  Please accept this offering.

Hail to Othala, Odal power.
  Please accept this offering."

Then recite the Aettir, or Anglo-Saxon Futhorc:

"Hail to Ear, hanging tree and grave.
  Please accept this offering.

Hail to Ac, who brings the gift of endurance.
  Please accept this offering.

Hail to Ior, guardian of boundaries.
  Please accept this offering.

Hail to Yr, discipline's teacher.
  Please accept this offering.

Hail to Os, God-voice and bard.
  Please accept this offering.

Hail to Cweorth, funeral pyre.
Please accept this offering.

Hail to Chalc, holy grail.
Please accept this offering.

Hail to Stan, mighty keystone.
Please accept this offering.

Hail to Gar, spear of Odin.
Please accept this offering.

I ask that you teach me your secrets and share your wisdom with me. In return, I give you this offering and promise to learn both wisely and well. Hail to the runes!"

VII. Final Prayer

Say:

"May what has been spoken here tonight,
Be writ into the web for all to see.

May Odin and my Ancestors bless and the Nornir stand witness.

Hail to the Gods. Hail to the runes.
This rite is ended."

Let the candles burn down of their own accord (at least the tea lights if the candles are too large).

3 The Elder Futhark

This is not a historical examination of the runes. There are numerous books available, many of which are listed in the Suggested Reading section, that serve that purpose. Rather, this is an exploration of the individual runes from the perspective of someone who has worked with them, both as a diviner and an occultist, for close to 20 years. The descriptions of the individual runes given below focus not on their history but on the physical, mental, spiritual, and richly metaphorical exegesis that is the rune-worker's purview alone. This is not to say that studying their historical context isn't useful; I believe it is both useful and necessary. But that is simply not what this book is about.

The most commonly used system of runes is called the Elder Futhark. This name is taken from the phonetic attributions of the first six runes when in their traditional positions: Fehu, Uruz, Thurisaz, Ansuz, Raido, and Kenaz. The Elder Futhark is typically divided into three *aettir*, or sets of eight. I have also included information on nine additional Anglo-Saxon and Northumbrian runes in the following chapter. These runes are not part of the Elder Futhark, but they are gaining in popularity. I know many rune-diviners who use these runes along with the Elder Futhark, but there is no rule that one must do this. The decision rests purely on personal preference.

To the rune-worker, each *aett* has its own distinctive character—spiritually, magically, and metaphorically. For instance, the first aett is a fiery, vibrant, intensely creative aett. That creative push forward, that drive that carries one into a state of inspiration that borders on the ecstatic, is the defining factor about this particular series of runes. They're primarily runes of initiation, initiation leading up to a metaphorical expression of Odin's ordeal. The second aett, in contrast, is much darker in feel and in usage. It speaks of the underworld, of the process of sacrifice, of death and rebirth. The third aett is very much a union of the two: knowledge gained and dearly paid for, manifesting in a clearly balanced, thought-out manner in Midgard. The order of the runes is important. They tell a story. They show a journey. They are the markers on the road.

Many modern rune books refer to the first aett as Frey or Freya's aett. This is a modern affectation that has little to do with the runes themselves. Although there is no historical evidence for this association, both Frey and Freya manifest the same type of golden, fiery, abundant, momentum-filled energy that the aett does, which may account for the attribution. Likewise, the second aett is often referred to as Hel's aett, Hel being the Goddess of the Underworld. Again, although this Goddess has no particular historical association with this aett, it speaks strongly of the mysteries of Her realm, of the Underworld, of passage into death, of transformation and rebirth. It is the same with the third aett, often called Tyr's aett. There is no historical reason for this attribution, but the feel of these eight runes is similar to that of Tyr—balanced detachment and applied wisdom hard won. That said, the first rune of this aett, Tiewaz, actually has a linguistic connection to the name of the warrior-God. In her book *Taking up the Runes*, Diana Paxson notes that "just as the word *ás* meant not only one of the Aesir, but specifically "the" god, Odin, the word *tyr*…could be used as a kenning for a god."[1]

Before we delve into the meanings of the individual runes, I want to again examine the way in which they were won. From a cosmological standpoint, the winning of the runes is told in the Runatal section of the Havamal. This poetic lay tells the story of Odin winning the runes and giving His eye for a drink from the Well of Inspiration and Memory. I have found meditation on these stanzas to be very beneficial to the novice rune-worker. One translation reads as follows:

> I know that I hung on a windy tree
> Nine long nights,
> Wounded with a spear, dedicated to Odin,
> Myself to myself,
> On that tree of which no man knows
> From where its roots run.
> No bread did they give me nor a drink from a horn,
> Downwards I peered;
> I took up the runes, screaming I took them,
> Then I fell back from there.
> Nine mighty spells I learnt from the famous son
> Of Bolthorn, Bestla's father,
> And I got a drink of the precious mead,
> Poured from Odroerir.
> Then I began to quicken and be wise,
> And to grow and to prosper;
> One word found another word for me,
> One deed found another deed for me."[2]

The tree in the above stanzas refers to Yggdrasil, the axis around which the Wyrd-web spins and which supports the nine worlds. It is the Tree of knowledge, the Tree of sacrifice, the Tree of the worlds. It is an eternal wellspring of cosmic power. This is the pathway to all the worlds and every hidden place within them, provided one has mastered the appropriate keys. All things resolve in and at the Tree. Odin opened those doors, making them available to those who might come after Him. He did this by willing, consciously chosen self-sacrifice to Himself. Although the stanzas read that He took up the runes, I've always thought it was more that He Himself was taken and penetrated by them, and then engaged with them in struggle for mastery. At any rate, this remains the defining moment of His mythos, and it is of great importance to understand this when one seeks to learn the runes and plumb their depths. To truly know them, the minutiae of this sacrifice must be understood on a personal, individual level.

After all, Odin's journey was his own, experiential and mystical. It was the ultimate unverified personal gnosis. Such things cannot be revealed or explained by words alone, but must be experienced by the individual. There is a point at which one must go into the darkness alone and make the choice of which doors to open and whether or not the attendant price is worth the knowledge gained. This is the wisdom of personal gnosis: It can only be truly understood by those who have shared the experience. Without the experience, there can be no true comprehension.

Odin is raw hunger—a hunger for wisdom, knowledge, and power—that will and can never be sated. He is hunger incarnate. The root of His name, *wodanaz*, means "fury" or "madness," and that is the deepest, darkest aspect of His nature. He can be a ravager; indeed, one of His most primal faces is that of a storm and wind God—raw and untamable, hungry and haunting, ravaging the land and any He finds unwitting in His path, stripping them bare and infusing them with that self-same hunger. As such, He is older than civilization and older than its mores. Yes, Odin has His civilized, highly cultured, even gentle facets. But He is ancient, and the rune-worker should never forget that whether he or she is dealing with Odin as healer, Shaman, king, or warrior, He was embodied hunger first—the exhalation of breath, the hunger for consciousness, the icy wind of the northern storm. Everything is a tool for Him. Everything is fodder to be offered up in sacrifice, with no exceptions. If Loki is, at times, a breaker of worlds (as many of His devotees assert), Odin is ravager of worlds. Before Him, no one else had dared to seek the runes. The price was simply too high.

After retelling Odin's story, the Havamal provides a guide for working with the runes effectively, warning:

> Do you know how to carve?
> Do you know how to interpret?
>
> Do you know how to stain?
> Do you know how to test out?
>
> Do you know how to ask?
> Do you know how to sacrifice?
>
> Do you know how to dispatch?
> Do you know how to slaughter?[3]

To my mind, this is perhaps the most infuriating, intriguing, and powerful passage in the whole Runatal. Historian Rudolf Simek lists the various actions (in order) as carving, advising, coloring (ostensibly with blood), asking, bidding, sending, and slaughtering.[4] He links this with sacrificing and the slaughter of animals in sacrificial *blot*, a word that is etymologically related to "blood." So this passage can be interpreted on many different levels, not just in the working of runes, but in the proper way to make a sacrifice and perform religious rituals, too.

There is a wonderful well-known quote by Balzac that sums up so many aspects of effective rune-work: "Power is not revealed by striking hard or striking often but in striking true."[5] In my early work with the runes, I interpreted the Havamal passage thusly: Do you know how to work the web of Wyrd and where to focus the magic? And do you know where to draw the power from to feed the casting? Do you know how to accurately interpret the shifting patterns of Wyrd? Do you know how to gain the help of Odin and the other Gods? Do you know how to call the rune-power into you and how to harness and use it? Do you know when to submit and when to seize control? Do you know how to use them to open the gates to the worlds? Do you know how to summon forth the power, and do you know exactly what you are willing to give of yourself to do so? And most importantly, are you strong enough to withstand the giving?

These are the things the vitki must learn and internalize through painstaking effort and study, often through trial and error. All rune-work is about balance—the balance within the vitki's personal Wyrd, the balance of elemental forces, and the balance of power given and received. The vitki must know when and what to cast, where to look, and how to interpret ever-shifting patterns. I cannot say it often enough: Rune-work is a process of reciprocity between oneself and the runes.

A note on the blank rune: Many modern rune sets include a blank rune, an inclusion that is based on some work of dubious historical and occult scholarship. There is no blank rune. Odin did not hang on the Tree for a blank rune. I do know of one Northern Traditionist who uses the blank rune and her reasoning is explored in Chapter 6. Even she, however, does not consider it part of the aettir or even a real rune. The use of the blank rune as part of the Elder Futhark was largely invented by Ralph Blum. The blank "rune" is mostly useful as a replacement tile in case you lose one. .

The First Aett

(Author's note: the associations I list at the end of each rune description have no historical precedent. They are based solely on my personal experience. For some people, carrying symbols of a rune and working with objects that call a particular rune to mind can be helpful. It can aid them in better understanding the rune's nature and how it can be called forth in Midgard. As you work with the runes you'll inevitably discover your own attributions, so please do not be limited by my small lists.)

Fehu

Anglo-Saxon name: Feoh

Phonetic equivalent: f

Traditional meaning: cattle, wealth (etymologically related to the English word "fee")

Anglo-Saxon rune poem:

> Feoh byþ frofur fira gehwylcum;
> sceal ðeah manna gehwylc miclun hyt dælan
> gif he wile for drihtne domes hleotan.

> Wealth is a comfort to all men;
> yet must every man bestow it freely,
> if he wish to gain honour in the sight of the Lord.[6]

Norwegian rune poem:

> Fé vældr frænda róge;
> føðesk ulfr í skóge.

> Wealth is a source of discord among kinsmen;
> the wolf lives in the forest.

Icelandic rune poem:

> Fé er frænda róg
> ok flæðar viti
> ok grafseiðs gata
> aurum fylkir.

> Wealth is a
> source of discord among kinsmen
> and fire of the sea
> and path of the serpent.

Modern rune poem by E. Vongvisith:[7]

Cattle die, they say,
but cattle are born too,
bought and sold, kept
or given away.
What value they have lies
not only in their giving or
owning, not only in meat,
milk, hide and hoof,
but in that which is invisible
to the most discriminating eye.
Know the worth of your kine,
both the herd and the ideas
that make it worth more than life,
more than sustenance, more
than perhaps you can afford.

Impressions of the rune

Luck, wealth, and rich, bubbling creative fire, it can be light in feel, almost quixotic. Fehu can help lighten depression. This is a rune of fine craftsmanship and the life spark. It is subtle but can manifest on many levels. It is also opportunity. Like a key turning in a thousand locks, it opens doors. By subtly changing the energy of one's Wyrd, a situation, or a relationship, it brings wealth and abundance. It expands; it is expansiveness itself. Though it is fire, it has a certain liquid quality in that it flows around and into everything. I often see it as a shower of gold. It is excitement and motivation. There is often a gleeful quality to this rune.

Fehu is about synergy. It's a rune of networking and creative connections. It can be cast to ease conflicts and may also have a beneficial effect in love-workings, though I wouldn't cast it as the primary rune in either love or healing; rather, I'd call upon it as a secondary power source, something that changes the shade of the energy. It uplifts the spirit and emotions. It is the rune of creative momentum and spirited negotiation. I have referred to it, tongue in cheek, as a metaphysical antidepressant. Fehu is the spark of attraction that leads to greater connection.

Fehu is a wellspring from which new ideas explode into being. In this sense it is a rune of inspiration. It is poetry, music, rhythm. It is a rune of beginnings. The image that comes to mind when I galdr Fehu is often of richly woven threads surging with liquid gold. This speaks to me of everything the God Andvari governs: responsibility, luck, and obligation with regard to right ownership (knowing what is yours by right and what is yours by accident, guarding your wealth, and allowing what is not yours to pass to its rightful owners). It is how one manages one's luck—the actions, words, and choices that strengthen or decrease it and one's *maegen*. Reversed, it indicates that something is negatively impacting maegen and luck. Or it might indicate dragon-disease—hoarding one's wealth wrongly, as Fafnir the dragon hoarded his gold, and not allowing it to grow, transform, or bring joy but killing it slowly by one's greed.

We carry Fehu in our blood cells. It surges through our capillaries, connecting us to our Ancestors and infusing our very veins with *hamingja*. Fehu reminds us of our connection to the Gods and that we were created by Them. It reminds us that while we are in this temporal form, some experiences will damage, pollute, or otherwise corrupt what the Gods put within us. For most of us, however, some parts are still just uncorrupted. I associate those parts with Fehu. It's those moments of "eureka" in the spiritual journey, those happy occurrences that balance out all the work we have to do in other areas spiritually. This rune can be very affirming and reassuring in this way.

Fehu facilitates self-appreciation, really understanding that your gifts were put there by the Gods. It also aids in discovering those hidden gifts. It makes you want to use those gifts to practical purpose. It makes you want to influence your environment and hamingja for the better. It has a contagious air to it, too: you want everyone else to experience the joy of recognizing their own gifts, as well.

When I think of Fehu, I also think of Odin going to the Tree. He had to go through a process of rebirth to win the runes. Even though He was a God before He went on the Tree, He had to go through this process. In the same way, we're not worms or slugs or down-in-the-dirt slaves because we have to go through spiritual struggles and trials and tribulations. We have value when we're "at Fehu," when we're just starting out. The other runes just increase that value. Fehu is self-knowledge; it's your core. It teaches you not to feel unworthy of the Gods. It teaches you your own value. In this, there is a strong connection to Freya's wisdom, which is knowing who you are and what you are worth. With that knowledge comes a natural unwillingness to compromise one's worth. This, too, is inherent in Fehu.

Fehu is also wealth and proper application and distribution of wealth and proper utilization of resources. Cattle were symbols of wealth for the Norse nearly as much as they were for the Celts, and this rune carries all of that symbology.

God(s)/Goddess(es) I associate with this rune:
 Frey, Freya, Vanic energies, and Andvari.

Miscellaneous associations:
 sunstone, marjoram, fennel, frankincense, heliotrope,
 citrine, aventurine, narcissus oil, coins, images of cows, gold.

Uruz

Anglo-Saxon name: Ur
Phonetic equivalent: u
Traditional meaning: aurochs

Anglo-Saxon rune poem:

> Ur byþ anmod ond oferhyrned,
> felafrecne deor, feohteþ mid hornum
> mære morstapa; þæt is modig wuht.

> The aurochs is proud and has great horns;
> it is a very savage beast and fights with its horns;
> a great ranger of the moors, it is a creature of
> mettle.

Norwegian rune poem:

> Úr er af illu jarne;
> opt løypr ræinn á hjarne.

> Dross comes from bad iron;
> the reindeer often races over the frozen snow.

Icelandic rune poem:

> Úr er skýja grátr
> ok skára þverrir
> ok hirðis hatr.
> umbre vísi

> Shower
> lamentation of the clouds
> and ruin of the hay-harvest
> and abomination of the shepherd.

Modern rune poem by E. Vongvisith:

> Mighty wild ox!
> Your hooves strike sparks
> and your broad horns stretch
> end to end farther than a man
> can reach out his arms.
> Your hair is long and woolly
> and your muscles thick.

Trampling, stamping,
blowing, bellowing, you
and your kin roam the world
in great herds, strong and free.

Show me how to withstand
and how to charge, unafraid
of the obstacles set before me.

Impressions of the rune

Uruz is sap; fire; growth; healing; raw, vital life energy; strength; fire; earth; and fire drawn from earth. It is an anchor. Because I associate this rune so strongly with grounding, I see it along with the root chakra as fire, primal energy of survival drawn from the depths of the earth. At the same time, Uruz doesn't always radiate heat to me; it can be a cool rune, a cleansing rune, soothing to inflammations of either the body or the spirit, or it can be a fire that burns so intensely it's beyond heat. I have often experienced this rune as very hot, but it's an odd heat. It has a force and weight to it like the flow of lava beneath the earth, or the solidity of the earth's core fire. There is a great deal of mountain energy in this rune, too, and it can be used to add immense stability to workings.

I have seen it come up reversed in divinatory spreads to indicate emotional blockages and areas in need of healing. It can also indicate a need for grounding in one's life. I see Uruz as a very good rune to meditate on in order to learn how to balance and translate one's spiritual and mystical experiences into the temporal realm. Of course, the strength and healing are more than just physical. It is a holistic rune, a rune of balance and harmony. It has more density than Fehu, and the quality of its energy is different— thicker and heavier.

Uruz is a rune of centeredness, restoration of the self, and healthy boundaries. It grants one the ability to remain unruffled, and the strength and stamina to endure. I see it as a great ancestral tree, deeply rooted yet expansively reaching up to the heavens. In this way, it is like a skeleton: it supports us energetically the way our bones support us physically. It's a drumbeat in the blood; it's the strength of body and bone; it runs in the marrow. It's the mighty roar of the ocean's waters, the thunder of the avalanche, the rushing hunger of the forest fire, in power if not elemental correspondence. It is expansive yet terribly solid.

This is a good rune for solidifying things. It's an excellent rune for learning how to work in Midgard, for integrating changes into one's mundane life, and for physical strengthening and healing. It can be used to dramatically increase the body's immune response. It is a rune of fighting—not the combat of the warrior, but the body's combat against infectious diseases.

I use this rune with Fehu and Berkana, occasionally Berkana and Sowelo or Berkana and Algiz, for overall health and healing. Uruz is a rune of boundaries and integrity of the self. It's also a rune of psychological and emotional healing. It will not permit one to escape into a fantasy world. It is a rune holistically grounded in reality, blended with the spiritual and the physical. Uruz eases tension and unblocks energy/chi. It gently amends clutter and clears away the old, the worn, and the unhealthy. It soothes what is jagged and breaks the cycle of pain so that healing can begin. It gives strength to lean upon in times of great crisis, pain, illness. It is a rune of balance and harmony.

A student of mine once mentioned that every time he meditated on Uruz, he heard the song "Sitting in My Place of Power," which actually makes a great deal of sense. Uruz is all about centered power. This rune can rejuvenate, heal, and nurture. When I meditate on it, I see the image of rich sap running through a huge tree into every branch and carrying life-giving essence. More than just healing the body, mind and spirit, it can restore the strength of the hamingja.

I also see Uruz as a rune of initiation, or, more to the point, of coming through initiation with the ability to apply what has been learned and what wisdom has been gained. There is a weight, a physicality, to this rune, but it is not a subjective physicality; it is dispassionate and objective. The ox, with its strength and stability, is a perfect symbol for Uruz. Because this is the wild ox (or the aurochs, which is extinct), Uruz is not associated with wealth in the way that Fehu is. Young men in ancient northern cultures used to have to hunt the aurochs as a coming-of-age ritual, so in this respect, Uruz is a rune of initiation and challenge, very powerfully so. Uruz is an immensely practical and pragmatic rune, very much like the Goddess Eir. In many respects the Norwegian rune poem points to this: one must be tempered, tested, challenged, and honed, just as metal is tested and tempered by being subjected to immense force and intense heat, in order for one to truly evolve. At the same time, this rune can help one find within oneself the endurance and courage to persevere through the worst challenges and ordeals.

Uruz is a very "terra firma" rune. It also gives you a sense of centeredness in the mundane things you have to do. This rune you can take anywhere. In addition to aiding your spiritual path and working with the Gods, it puts everything, even getting up and going to work, in its proper place. It's very much about being in the here and now. It centers you so that you can make yourself whole and functional. When spiritual or magical work leaks negatively into mundane areas, Uruz comes very strongly to remedy those situations. It would be a good rune to use when you are overloaded and hung over from too much seidhr. It would also be excellent for surviving Shaman sickness.

Uruz connects the many different layers and levels of being-ness we have to traverse. It is an incredibly holistic, no-nonsense rune. Uruz can be very healing and stabilizing, but if you go into it with preexisting values or opinions regarding your spiritual or mundane makeup, you won't get its full benefits. Uruz balances. It takes everything and says, "This is the way it should be." If you go into it holding onto something and insisting that it take a certain place in your life, it won't work; you have to give Uruz everything and let *it* create the balance. You can't go into it 100-percent certain where your equilibrium is coming from, because most of the time it's not where you would think. Uruz will show you your true center. It challenges you to let go of the illusions of equilibrium that you have created for yourself.

God(s)/Goddess(es) I associate with this rune:
> Eir, Sunna, Arvolecia, and Alateivia.

Miscellaneous associations:
> sycamore, maple, sap, wintergreen oil, basil, green tea, granite. Years ago, I used to associate jasper and bloodstone with this rune, but now I would be more inclined to say nephrite or jade.

Thurisaz

Traditional meaning: giant
Anglo-Saxon name: thorn
Phonetic equivalent: <u>th</u>

Anglo-Saxon rune poem:

> Ðorn byþ ðearle scearp; ðegna gehwylcum
> anfeng ys yfyl, ungemetum reþe
> manna gehwelcum, ðe him mid resteð.

> The thorn is exceedingly sharp,
> an evil thing for any knight to touch,
> uncommonly severe on all who sit among them.

Norwegian rune poem:

> Þurs vældr kvinna kvillu;
> kátr værðr fár af illu.

> Giant causes anguish to women;
> misfortune makes few men cheerful.

Icelandic rune poem:

> Þurs er kvenna kvöl
> ok kletta búi
> ok varðrúnar verr.
> Saturnus þengill.

> Giant
> torture of women
> and cliff-dweller
> and husband of a giantess.

Modern rune poem by E. Vongvisith:

> The way is long and dark
> through the brambles, and
> the thorn tears cloth and flesh
> with equal savage ferocity,

> the way an angry wolf
> lunges, heedless of self,
> seeking only pain.

> But unlike the wolf, this is
> a small thing, though painful
> and greater in great numbers.

> Soon the thicket ends and
> you push through to sunlight,
> clear air, space and forest.

Impressions of the rune

Thurisaz is a great rune, but it has an incredibly destructive power. It destroys illusions, brings underlying conflicts to the fore, clears away obstacles, and opens doors. I have a friend in my kendo class who wears Thurisaz as a personal rune. I thought the guy terribly misguided at first until I talked with him and meditated on it. My friend has incredibly wild, extroverted energy. It's all over the place and almost too expansive. He started working with Thurisaz as a way of honing that energy, pulling it all in and focusing it with narrow, surgical precision—all without losing one iota of its force or power. Because of him, I learned that Thurisaz can be used like a laser.

Thurisaz has the ability to be wielded with the precision of a surgeon's scalpel cutting away a cancerous growth. It can also be extremely potent sexual energy or simply ferocious destruction and conflict. It is a most dangerous rune, but I believe that this is largely because it is misunderstood and feared. Thurisaz cannot be wielded by one who fears its power. It is a hungry rune—a very hungry rune. It likes to attack and devour. It has no conscience. It can be devious and outright destructive. It cannot be approached with anxiety or fear.

I could see thurisaz being used in healing in extreme cases, much as chemotherapy is used to heal cancer. It is neither good nor evil, but powerful—a thing of chaos (but chaos with a purpose, as without chaos there is no growth). I've been warned to be extremely careful when using it on women because some rune-healers believe it can have very negative effects on women's reproductive organs.

Thurisaz breaks down boundaries and shakes things up emotionally speaking. This is not necessarily a bad thing, as it can provide a powerful time to clear out entropy, what pulls you down and sucks your energy (unhealthy behavior patterns, for example). It can provide a powerful opportunity for self-examination and growth, in the same way one shatters a geode to see the gems inside. It's not a comfortable rune in any sense. It is a swift, uncontained force. It's not evil or malicious, but it possesses a dark exuberance that can wreak havoc if not properly balanced and tempered. If tempered, it can bring about precise destruction the same way a jeweler cuts facets in a diamond. Given free reign, however, it can leave searing destruction in its wake.

Thurisaz is especially good at bringing hidden issues and untruths to blazing light. It will ferret them out and reveal them in the most unexpected of ways. It has a keen, cunning awareness. It's like a tank that pushes through blockages and bad situation—very raw, primal, "survival of the fittest" energy. It causes damage and rends one emotionally, spiritually, and physically. It brings about shocking epiphanies in the wake of its destruction. It's also a powerful defensive rune and thus should be in every warrior's arsenal. It is cataclysmic. It can also be cast to break through a person's defenses.

Thurisaz can grant one the fortitude to walk into spiritual and emotional infernos and come out whole, if a bit battered. It's a rune of stubborn, aggressive endurance. It isn't passive in any way. It can help one create change in one's life but it does not do this gently. I have used this rune in aggressive cleansings, but never by itself. With regard to the hamingja, Thurisaz has the power to violently cleanse it, searing and scraping it clean, but it is a painful, disruptive cleansing.

This is a killing rune. Like a virus in the blood, it can maneuver itself into a person's Wyrd, devouring and destroying everything in its wake. I can see how it could easily drive a person mad. It is jagged in feel and it creates the same in those it strikes. Because it's a physical rune, it can be exceptionally good for athletes and martial artists to meditate on, but it must be grounded and balanced by other work.

Thurisaz is the manifestation of that unique force within you that demands expression. It's the culmination of all those energies that enable you to be the artist, the warrior, the athlete, and so on. It rune is so raw it can't be expressed by itself, so it is expressed through all our passions, including sexual passion. This rune is the embodiment of sexual lust.

It's important not to limit your emotions with Thurisaz. It's easy to allow anger and rage to come out with this rune; indeed, it takes those emotions very well and feeds on them, but there is more to Thurisaz than that. It can just as easily take exuberance, enthusiasm, and passion—a lot of passion, especially. The key here, and what this rune teaches you, is not allowing these things to control you. It makes a very good servant but a very, very bad master. If the world was created, as it says in the Eddas, in a conflagration of ice and fire, Thurisaz was that moment and force of the collision.

There's a core of control that runs through Thurisaz. It takes everything, but doesn't take when you're willing to give. For instance, it can take rage, but you just can't throw rage anywhere you like and say, "Here, Thurisaz, take it." It won't do that. It forces you to give in certain areas and at certain times; it pulls it out of you by forcing you to go into parts of your psyche you may not be comfortable exploring. Thurisaz challenges you to express difficult emotions such as rage and anger in ways that will be of greatest benefit to you in outcome. It's not enough to be able to plumb those emotions to cast Thurisaz; it's also necessary to explore and work with those emotions. It forces you to see those emotions as clay to be molded.

Someone once asked me what the key is to safely working Thurisaz. My response was that you have to find that energy inside yourself, be comfortable with it, and know how to give it positive outlets. If there is any fear at all, it's best not to touch Thurisaz. This is a completely amoral rune, and it will just as readily feed on your fear as that of your opponent.

God(s)/Goddess(es) I associate with this rune:
   Loki, Thor, and Farbauti.

Miscellaneous associations:
   Jotuns, muspellheim, destruction, burning core of the
   earth, comets, fire, dark carnelian, jasper, jalap, dragon's

blood, burnt orange, rust, red, spikenard, tiger's eye, iron, blades, gunpowder, tiger iron, hot peppers, broken glass, rose thorns, blackthorn, and hawthorn.

Ansuz

Traditional meaning: mouth, God

Anglo-Saxon name: Os

Phonetic equivalent: \a\

Anglo-saxon rune poem:

> Os byþ ordfruma ælere spræce,
> wisdomes wraþu ond witena frofur
> and eorla gehwam eadnys ond tohiht.

> The mouth is the source of all language,
> a pillar of wisdom and a comfort to wise men,
> a blessing and a joy to every knight.

Norwegian rune poem:

> Óss er flæstra færða
> for; en skalpr er sværða.

> Estuary is the way of most journeys;
> but a scabbard is of swords.

Icelandic rune poem:

> Óss er algingautr
> ok ásgarðs jöfurr,
> ok valhallar vísi.

> God, aged Gautr
> and prince of Ásgarðr
> and lord of Vallhalla.

Modern rune poem by E. Vongvisith:

> From the high mountaintops,
> from the verdant hills,
> across the crown of
> the echoing forest,
> across the crested white waves
> comes a Voice.
>
> Hear it
> in the passing word of a stranger.
> Listen for it
> behind the pulse of your own heartbeat.
> Seek it
> in silence between speeches
> and the pause before the beginning
> of a long, densely woven song.
>
> A message comes to you.
> Open eyes and ears
> to the gods who speak
> with tones loud as an avalanche,
> soft as a feather's fall.

Impressions of the rune

This rune helps one find one's voice. It opens the way for purification and cleansing. On a purely practical level, I've used it to unclog my toilet and, when reversed, to bind a broken pipe. I've used it to unlock sticky doors and, reversed, to lock them again. It is the attention and breath of Odin, and it washes away all that binds the spirit and the consciousness. It is a key that opens any door, a furious host of warriors riding into battle at Odin's side—it is the metaphorical cry of the Valkyries in battle. It expands consciousness and awareness. It is the first rune of Odin, for it is a prelude to any journeying and shamanic work. Reversed, it can bind. As breath of

Odin it is also the breath cord, a connection to the most primal of Ancestors—the Gods who brought us to life, and Ask and Embla, the first proto-people. It's as primal as fire. It binds us to everything—to being, to knowing, to the aether, and to the Gods Themselves. It is the fury of the storm and the raging wind, or Odin as Wodenaz.

Ansuz eases what Thurisaz opens, clearing away the debris by creating smooth flow. Its energy runs the gamut from a gentle breeze to the force of a hurricane gale. It clears the way for us to step up and act consciously as cocreators with the Gods. It helps free us of unhealthy bonds, codependency, and unhealthy attachments. It does this by allowing us to clearly see these things in ourselves. Reversed, it can bind up quite tightly but it does not harm. It's dispassionate and removed from what is being bound. It can help bring objectivity in counseling, and enables us to hear the voice of the Gods.

Ansuz is the unbinder, that which cuts through all facades and brings clarity and understanding. It heralds movement on the mental and spiritual levels, and overcomes obstacles. I don't associate this rune with emotion; rather, it's the means to transcend the turmoil of one's emotions (though sometimes there is a certain abandon of "battle joy" in it and of riding unfettered through a raging storm). I associate this rune with air because, like air, it permeates everything and is necessary to life. Ansuz opens all doors, reveals all secrets, moves beyond the merely temporal. It is a highly magical rune. Through Ansuz, one may learn how to find and link into the patterns of galdr-chant and how to vocally weave the Wyrd-web itself. It helps one gain one's voice. I see spears flying through the air with this rune; it has the power to tear asunder any magical weapons thrown at you. As such, it is associated with Odin riding into battle with the Valkyries at His side.

I have occasionally cast Ansuz as a healing rune because it can open energy blockages, relieve tension, unknot sore muscles, and so on. However it is not a "warm" rune. I find its primary purpose is to break through bonds, especially magical ones. It opens the channels of magic. Reversed in a reading, it can indicate a mental blockage or unwillingness to face reality. Used properly, Ansuz can enhance one's ability to sense and use power and can stir up reservoirs of power. I often see Odin's ravens when this rune is cast. If Uruz is mountain energy, Ansuz is the energy of the storm and the excitement of standing in the eye of a storm. It sweeps away what is outmoded, decayed, or brittle. It is a rune of renewal. It raises understanding and intellect to the spiritual level, because it is a rune of far sight and strategy.

Ansuz can bring a total shattering revelation about the Gods or one's spirituality such that it results in the shedding of tears. These tears aren't necessarily connected to an emotion; rather, they are cleansing tears. Ansuz comes to pave the way for later work. It brings awareness that the Gods are there waiting for us. The tears I associate with Ansuz come from an immense cleansing of the soul. It's a very challenging rune, a difficult rune to access. It's a no-nonsense, no-half-measures, all-or-nothing rune. You can't barter with Ansuz. It knows exactly where it needs to go and what it needs to do. You have to really work with this rune.

Ansuz occupies its place in the Futhark order for a reason. A great deal can be done with Ansuz (and with the runes that come after it) if it's fully understood in its context. For this reason, I would recommend working with Ansuz for a long time before moving onto the other runes. As Yggdrasil connects all the worlds, we all have a spiritual core that connects all the different "worlds" within. Ansuz cleans that spiritual core. The other runes will force you to focus on one or more of these "worlds," but if you haven't worked enough with Ansuz to clean that core you won't be able to easily travel the pathways the other runes want to explore. Ansuz goes through all the pathways. It's an excellent general cleansing.

Ultimately, Ansuz represents the sacred breath Odin breathed into us, giving us life. It's not just air but raging, furious, roaring hurricane wind. It is both tamed and untamable, depending on its mood. Ansuz also has to do with the power of words and, by extension, the swearing of oaths.

God(s)/Goddess(es) I associate with this rune:
   Odin.

Miscellaneous associations:
   wind, storms, binding and loosening of fetters, galdr, singing, ash tree, Yggdasil, spears (specifically, Odin's spear), ravens, feathers, grey, blue, mistletoe, fennel, certain forms of calcite, fluorite, Herkimer diamonds, blades, clearing obstacles, words (written and spoken), galdr, song, sacred chant.

Raido
Traditional meaning: riding
Anglo-Saxon name: Rad
Phonetic equivalent: \r\

Anglo-Saxon rune poem:

   Rad byþ on recyde rinca gehwylcum
   sefte ond swiþhwæt, ðamðe sitteþ on ufan
   meare mægenheardum ofer milpaþas.

   Riding seems easy to every warrior while he is indoors
   and very courageous to him who traverses the high-roads
   on the back of a stout horse.

Norwegian rune poem:

> Ræið kveða rossom væsta;
> Reginn sló sværðet bæzta.

> Riding is said to be the worst thing for horses;
> Reginn forged the finest sword.

Icelandic rune poem:

> Reið er sitjandi sæla
> ok snúðig ferð
> ok jórs erfiði
> iter ræsir.

> Riding
> joy of the horsemen
> and speedy journey
> and toil of the steed.

Modern rune poem by E. Vongvisith:

> The road beckons.
> Beyond the next curve
> lies the wonder.
> Find your face
> in the faces of those you meet
> along the road.
> Find your self
> in the omens and signs
> that point you along the way.
> Find your fate
> waiting over distant hills,
> on the other side of the sea,
> or just down the block.

> The road beckons.
> Why are you still at home?

Strike out and follow
where all the other footprints
have worn a dusty track
into the solemn earth.

Impressions of the rune

Raido is a rolling forward. It pushes over obstacles, seizes opportunities. It is an expansion of vision; it has momentum, a release of tension like an arrow shot from a bow (but not so sharp and narrow in its focus). It brings strategic sight and the ability to see long-term goals. It is movement from one state of being to another, but it's more of a lateral movement than an upward trajectory. This rune can get you out of trouble.

Raido is a rune of journeying. It is powerful forward motion that surpasses any obstacles. It can indicate strong spiritual movement/opening. It is a rune of arising after a spiritual descent. I usually cast this rune by adding it to other combinations of runes to give power and push to the spell. When combined with Tiewaz and Jera, it has the power to bring Wyrd down on one's head. It has definite repercussions on the web of Wyrd as it tends to crisscross the web. I suspect this rune could be used reversed to drain someone's hamingja. There is nothing static with this particular rune; even at rest, it vibrates and hums with a kinetic power all its own. It is energy in forward motion. It is not power held, but rather, power that was previously coiled but has now been released like a bullet shot from a pistol. It links into the changing currents of the web itself. Raido can move one out of spiritual ruts. However, it is not a breaking rune; you will need another rune for that. It is the flow that comes after the dam has burst. It's not a "flat on your back" spiritual awakening; rather, it's riding the waves of enlightenment that come from spiritual awakening. An extremely practical rune, it works equally well in mundane and spiritual matters. It works especially well in matters pertaining to work and career.

God(s)/Goddess(es) I associate with this rune:
Gna, Loki.

Miscellaneous associations:
movement, wagon, wheel, horse, moss agate, iolite, brown agate, meteorites, chariot card in Tarot.

 ## Kenaz

Traditional meaning: torch
Anglo-Saxon name: Ken
Phonetic Value: \k\

Anglo-Saxon rune poem:
Cen byþ cwicera gehwam, cuþ on fyre
blac ond beorhtlic, byrneþ oftust
ðær hi æþelingas inne restaþ.

The torch is known to every living man by its pale, bright flame;
it always burns where princes sit within.

Norwegian rune poem:
Kaun er barna bolvan;
bol gørver nán folvan.

Ulcer is fatal to children;
death makes a corpse pale.

Icelandic Rune Poem
Kaun er barna böl
ok bardaga [för]
ok holdfúa hús.
flagella konungr.

Ulcer
disease fatal to children
and painful spot
and abode of mortification.

Modern rune poem by E. Vongvisith:

O fire of revelations!
O thou, bringer of clarity
through the hammer's constant fall,
forging the hot iron core
of what is essential,
strike after strike shaping
the bright two-edged blade.

Your name sings itself
into the making of that which
cannot be ignored or denied for long
in the darkness lighted by your shaping,
by your steady completion
in the hands of a true craftsman.

For truth is the substance
melted down for this forge,
truth is the bellows' sigh
that feeds the inferno,
truth the invincible weapon
for good or bane,
laid aside to await its turn to fight.

Impressions of the rune

Kenaz gives one the ability to manifest intellectual endeavors. It makes the theoretical real. It is light rather than fire, a gentle illumination on all levels. It illuminates truth and contains all kennings. It symbolizes the eternal flame of the spirit. It is a rune of mental dexterity and also magical and shamanic dexterity (including shape-changing). It is the warmth of a welcoming, well-kept, spiritually whole hearth, the symbolic center of the home. It is a rune of hallowing, including hallowing of the spirit. It is also a rune of centering and of health. Kenaz can be a rune of consecration and of hospitality, and can ward away negative energy. It sanctifies a dwelling, as fire by its very nature cleanses.

Kenaz is a rune of the fruition of ideas. The creative fire raised by Fehu is honed and made manifest through Kenaz. It is also the rune of the solar plexus, the seat of the will. It can help take the bite out of anger, and can teach us how to use our anger instead to uncover untruths and identify circumstances that must be changed. Through Saga, it is the rune of lore-keeping, study, memory, record-keeping, and genealogy. It is a good rune to use to begin ancestral work (so is Othila, though Kenaz is more personal in feel). Given its linguistic connection to the word "kin," it is also the spiritual connection to our Ancestors, the cord through which their wisdom can flow freely down to us.

Kenaz is a very important rune to use in any type of shamanic journey. It is the torch, the spark of consciousness, that guides us through inner darkness. It is the spark of the divine within. It is the knowledge that enables one to adequately use the information gained in one's journey. I see it as a rune of fine craftsmanship, care in one's work, and patient crafting. It is the rune of teachers, the presence of Deity, the immanent awakening or kindling of the magical will. It is a rune of connections on all levels. I saw it once as Odin's eye, plucked out and offered in exchange for wisdom; as such, it may be a key to clarity and awareness of all kinds. It gives one the ability to see within and to see through facades, as well as the will to seek out knowledge and experience. It is will, raised above the mere scrabbling for physical achievements.

Kenaz is also connected to totems in the form of animals, plants, or stones. It provides a means of reaching them, working with them, and communicating with them respectfully. Far warmer than Ansuz, this rune brings clarity to mixed emotions and confusion. Conversely, when cast reversed, it may cloud inner vision and lock one down both magically and astrally.

It has come up in my readings to indicate relationships, friendships more often than romances. It may also indicate the balanced responsibilities and give-and-take of a strong, positive teacher-student relationship. It may indicate opportunities for growth and learning. It can also presage an intense spiritual awakening.

Eventually, somewhere within your spiritual landscape, you will find Kenaz. At some point, you have to find it and protect it at all costs. This is a disastrous rune to have snuffed out—deadly, in fact. It is a very personal, very spiritual rune. Whatever you put into it is beyond invaluable. It controls so many fundamental components of life and spiritual awareness. It's so illuminating; without it, there is only darkness and despair. We need Kenaz because it guides us and shows us where it is we need to go and, more importantly, where we should not go. This is its connection with Heimdall, the Watchman of Asgard. It makes right connections glow. When you encounter something that you just know is important to your spiritual makeup (that feeling of "this is right, this is something I need to do or learn"), that's Kenaz. People who have "good" Kenaz and "bad" Kenaz are diametrically opposed. It's like comparing heaven and hell. It's a rune you must have in order, clean and strong. You can't ignore Kenaz.

God/desses I associate with this rune:
> Odin, Heimdall, Saga, Sif, Weyland.

Miscellaneous associations:
> fire, enlightenment, learning, scholarship, kinship bonds, torch, Odin's eye, topaz, citrine, tiger's eye, frankincense, broom, tobacco, kinship with the Gods.

Gebo

Traditional meaning: gift

Anglo-Saxon name: Gifu

Phonetic Value: \g\

Anglo-Saxon Rune Poem:

> Gyfu gumena byþ gleng and herenys,
> wraþu and wyrþscype and wræcna gehwam
> ar and ætwist, ðe byþ oþra leas.

> Generosity brings credit and honor, which
> support one's dignity;
> it furnishes help and subsistence
> to all broken men who are devoid of aught else.

There are no Icelandic or Norwegian rune poems for Gebo.

Modern rune poem by E. Vongvisith:

> Two paths cross, two hands meet,
> two lives intersect, two clans join.
> From one road to another,
> from one hand to another,
> from one life to another,
> from one folk to another
> comes the gift of great worth.

> Because no crossroads has an end
> and no hands act alone,
> no lives go unshared
> and no clans exist without renewal,
> so it is bound to be given
> from one road to another
> from one hand to another,
> from one life to another,
> from one folk to another—
> another gift of great worth.

Impressions of the rune

This rune is an "epic" rune that is unique to each person. It's a long journey and so much goes into it. It's the ineffable spiritual and life journey each person takes. I say "ineffable" because there are often no words to describe this journey. For example, we can say that Odin hung on the Tree, but words do not adequately express that experience. It is a crossroads, an incredibly powerful rune to use in shamanic journeying. When used to curse, it brings all Wyrd home to roost, and the "victim" literally curses him- or herself with the consequences of his or her poor actions. It is union by oath, contract, heart, and/or spirit. It can be used for either positive or negative purposes. In shamanic journeying it can teach how to traverse worlds and also how to appropriately use one's tools. It marks the presence of the Gods, bringing a gift of magic and awareness.

Through Oski (Odin as "Gift-Bringer"), it brings the gift of growth. It teaches us to seek out energy sources and use our gifts to the best of our ability. Through Yggr (Odin as the "Terrible One"), this is the rune of spiritual and emotional challenges, of the spiritual descent. Gebo is the rune of kinetic balance achieved by many necessary adjustments: Odin handing on the Tree, in pain and bleeding, as the runes were being formed. Gebo helps us understand the work that true balance requires. It's not something that's achieved and static, but rather, something you work at for eternity in an ever-shifting dance. That's where the gift part comes in, because you're constantly giving and receiving to get to that balance while it's constantly changing.

Sacrifice is involved in Gebo. Blood is involved in Gebo. It ties into Odin on the Tree: mystical, sacred shamanic sacrifice and the resulting awareness. Gebo may look nice on the surface, so much so that it can easily be dismissed. In reality, however, there's a lot of effort and struggle in Gebo. It takes great strength and power to maintain the balance in its shape.

We use every bit of blood, sweat, and tears, to etch out our own Gebo. Part of its power involves being willing to share Odin's place on the Tree.

Gebo encompasses that world of exchange. In ancient Norse societies (and in modern Heathenry), the dominant culture was a gift-giving one. In this context, gift-giving can be seen as a martial art. It can even be a form of violence in its own way. This is why the Havamal cautions us: "'Tis better not to give than to give too much, for a gift demands a gift."[8] Gift-giving creates intense bonds of obligation between people, and it can be used to reinforce social and familial roles and connections. Gift-giving is its own type of conversation. It's is a way to create, balance, and alter social power and hierarchy. It's also a form of recognition of position, power, and influence. One can even give a gift as a form of challenge. This is why gift-giving was a very public part of certain rites and rituals in ancient Norse cultures. It's all about hierarchy, status and pride. Social bonds aren't always friendly, and depending how Gebo is aspected in a reading, this may be its necessary warning. This rune embodies that whole unseen power in the giving of a gift.[9]

Gift-giving isn't always grim, however. Gebo can also indicate balanced partnership and equal give-and-take, the exchange evident in a good marriage partnership. In many ways, the exchange of Gebo is integral to the maintenance of social fabric, whether that exchange is social, emotional, physical, or magical. That is its usual interpretation today, though it is Gebo in its "lightest," least demanding aspect. Gebo is that which demands a price, the energy involved in paying that price, and receiving in exchange. It is the acknowledgement that a gift is indeed a dangerous thing.

God(s)/Goddess(s) I associate with this rune:

Oski, Ygg, and Hangagod (all aspects of Odin).

Miscellaneous associations:
wind, earth, ash tree, yew tree, Yggdrasil, sacrifice, exchange of gifts, the gift of love/friendship, Odin's sacrifice on the Tree, the Wild Hunt, cross stones, sugilite.

Wunjo

Traditional meaning: joy, perfection
Anglo-Saxon name: Wynn
Phonetic equivalent: \w\ or \v\

Anglo-saxon rune poem:

Wenne bruceþ, ðe can weana lyt
sares and sorge and him sylfa hæfþ
blæd and blysse and eac byrga geniht.

Bliss he enjoys who knows not suffering,
sorrow nor anxiety,
and has prosperity and happiness and a good
enough house.

There are no Icelandic or Norwegian rune poems for Wunjo.

Modern rune poem by E. Vongvisith:

Alight,
alive,
that burst of crystal illumination,
that steady glow
pierces every darkness,
warms the forsaken soul,
casts away dread and glosses
even the dimmest night
with a sparking sheen of hope.

Its glow warms the heart
locked in shadowy gloom.
Its light points the way
out of the tangles, overgrown wood.
Its banner unfolds under
the pure sky of a new day.

Rejoice,
because, though the suffering
may not yet abate,
its end is in sight,
vanquished soon by happiness

Impressions of the rune

This rune can bring a passionate blending of consciousness with the Divine. In this, it is the mystic's rune. It is the ecstasy— the shamanic trance, joy, and even madness—that neither the body nor the mind can contain, and which makes us "fools for God." It is passing through the point of sacrifice to unite with Odin on the other side of the Tree. It is awareness, and living in many realities, planes, and times at once. It is a gift of passionate love and union. It is a gift of magic. When I see Wunjo, it glitters. It is a wedding of one's heart, mind, and spirit to one's God. It opens the crown chakra to that gift of awareness and magic more precious than diamonds. It is the experience of standing on the pinnacle of power, leadership, and joy that comes with union with Deity.

This is a difficult rune for me to write about, though I connect with it strongly. I almost see it and Gebo as a pair. I also associate it with the crown chakra, the point of connection of our higher selves with the Gods. It is representative of your innermost spirit. You become like the Tree with this rune, drinking up nourishment from the soil (the soil being your spiritual work and the sum total of your life's endeavors, your striving to be better, to grow, and to evolve). It represents all your magical and spiritual gifts. It is your potential. The process of offering those things to the Gods, and the Gods taking those gifts and blessing you in return—that's Wunjo.

It's a very joyous rune, but that joy comes from recognizing your own self-worth almost as much as the Gods do. It's seeing in yourself all the magic, power, beauty, strength, wisdom, and potential that the Gods do. It is a very beautiful rune. You're not thrown into the throes of struggle as you are with Gebo; Wunjo is beyond that. It almost has a seductive quality to it. Wunjo can be very sweet. As I do with Fehu, I see *odhroerir*, the poetic mead, with this rune, but it's deeper, more potent, and more intensely passionate. When used with other runes such as Mannaz, Wunjo can be a rune of the sacred marriage.

Negatively, Wunjo is a sickle that cuts the threads that connect you to the Deities. Magical and mystical connection to Deity is very important with Wunjo. Ironically, the desire to experience the intensity of emotions and feelings associated with Wunjo can prevent you from experiencing it fully. If you approach this rune expecting ecstasy you'll never completely understand it. Wunjo happens almost instantaneously. Unlike Gebo, which takes effort and time, Wunjo takes you through many struggles at once; this is where the inspiration comes from. It's like being in darkness and suddenly having a veil lifted off your eyes: You suddenly see clearly where you saw nothing before.

Each rune has its shadow aspect that is far darker than a reversal. With Wunjo, it's madness, insanity, and the making of one lawful prey. Wunjo is present when ecstasy spirals into obsession, when inspiration becomes insanity, when joy turns to delusion. Just as its positive face is one of balance and *bhakti*, its negative face is one of extremes and excess.

God(s)/Goddess(s) I associate with this rune:
    Odin (as Wunsch, Oski, or All-Father), Vali. Other rune-
    workers see Frigga (as a Wyrd-worker) strongly with this rune.

Miscellaneous associations:
   magic, ecstasy, mastery, ownership, possession, ecstatic
   trance, Deity possession, sexual ecstasy, spindle, spear,
   wand, kunzite, lepidolite, pinkish-lavender, wedding ring,
   madness, fly agaric.

The Second Aett

The first aett is about motivation, cleansing, and markers
on the journey. The second aett takes us down into the underworld, into the unconscious, into the moments that span the
space between start and finish of the act of sacrifice itself. It is
a very internal process. This is a terrible aett—in the ancient
sense of the word as terror-and awe -inspiring. Odin died on
the Tree when He hung for the runes. This aett contains the
story of His journey during the time between His dying and
His renewal. This is the aett which ensures that one does not
come through such a journey unchanged.

Hagalaz

Traditional meaning: hail

Anglo-Saxon name: Haegl/Hagal

Phonetic value: H

Anglo-Saxon rune poem:
   Hægl byþ hwitust corna; hwyrft hit of
   heofones lyfte,
   wealcaþ hit windes scura; weorþeþ hit to
   wætere syððan.

   Hail is the whitest of grain;
   it is whirled from the vault of heaven
   and is tossed about by gusts of wind
   and then it melts into water.

Norwegian rune poem:

> Hagall er kaldastr korna;
> Kristr skóp hæimenn forna.

> Hail is the coldest of grain;
> Christ created the world of old.[10]

Icelandic rune poem:

> Hagall er kaldakorn
> ok krapadrífa
> ok snáka sótt.
> grando hildingr.

> Hail
> cold grain
> and shower of sleet
> and sickness of serpents.

Modern rune poem by E. Vongvisith:

> You crash through rooftops,
> hammering, breaking down
> this man's house and not the other's
> less than a field away.

> You fall burning
> from the sky, hunks of charred metal
> and smoking bodies; some live,
> some do not.

> You scream by in a whir
> of blue and red lights—
> today for another,
> tomorrow, perhaps, for me.

> I watch the storm coming,
> bearing its load of hail,
> and there is no way to know
> if the tender grain-stalks will survive.

Impressions of the rune

I always associate this rune with Hella and the journey to Her realm. It's the rune of spiritual descent. It stirs up the subconscious and dredges up issues we often repress. It takes us into the darkest realms of our spirit and psyche, forcing us to deal with every hidden emotion, every façade, every hurt, every weakness—everything about us that we would consider less than positive. It's very definitely a rune of shadow-work. Mother issues can often arise when working with this particular rune, as well. It's also a rune of shamanic journeying to the underworld, and of *seidhr*, a type of sorcery. It can be cast to absorb negative and/or malignant energy. It often comes up in readings when a very difficult or shocking truth is about to be revealed.

Hagalaz is a rune of passages, including the passage of the dead from this realm to Helheim. It can enable one to connect with the dead very easily. With Hagalaz, there is a great deal of raw material to work with. It can be a very comforting rune if one is fairly comfortable with oneself. I consider this very much a rune of the "dark night of the soul" that the Christian mystics spoke of and which is such an integral part of any intense spirituality. It's the shaman's journey into the dark unknown, especially the unknown within. It is a rune of solitude and solitary seeking.

It can be a positive rune in that it enables one to sift through the past to craft a strong present and future. In this way, I like to meditate on Hagalaz with Berkana. This combination is immensely rich spiritually, like a soft, warm cloak in an icy winter rain. It is a rune that can be used to connect to one's *Disir*, or female Ancestors. Hagalaz can help bring to light all those things we hide or tuck away—buried pain, loss, grief, and anger—bringing them out into awareness so that we can deal effectively with them. It's an intensely contemplative rune, rather like a gentle tide at moonrise: quiet and soothing, yet with an intense clarity that is all the more penetrating for its subtlety. It can sooth jagged emotions by getting to their source. It's a rune of winter, of darkness, of silence, of healing. It is a rich rune, full of promise. For all its promise, however, Hagalaz can be a dark and tricky rune. The first vertical line is where you begin, the second is where you need to go, and the center line is the path to get from one place to the other. You'll notice that it's slanted, not straight, which is one of this rune's lessons: you can't always go straight into things, and your course in life is often only revealed as you're going through it, not before. This is what connects it to shamanism. Hagalaz teaches us to find meaning in the journey itself.

In the occult, the element of Water is associated with the subconscious, deep emotions, and psychic phenomena. All of that is bound up in this rune. Just as water, when frozen into hail, can cause immense damage, this rune takes things that normally don't have much power and imbues them with a potential for destruction. It works on an internal level by creating disruptions. Hagalaz is a very inventive rune.

God(s)/Goddess(s) I associate with this rune:
    Hella, the Ancestors (particularly the Disir). Others see
    Frigga with this rune.

Miscellaneous associations:
    mandrake, henbane, nightshade, Helheim, rock
    crystal, black goldstone, ice, hail, spiritual descent, the
    subconscious, fog, dark places.

Nauthiz
Traditional meaning: need

Anglo-Saxon name: Nyd

Phonetic equivalent: \n\

Anglo-Saxon rune poem:

> Nyd byþ nearu on breostan; weorþeþ hi þeah
> oft niþa bearnum
> to helpe and to hæle gehwæþre, gif hi his
> hlystaþ æror.

> Trouble is oppressive to the heart;
> yet often it proves a source of help and salvation
> to the children of men, to everyone who heeds
> it betimes.

Norwegian rune poem:

> Nauðr gerer næppa koste;
> nøktan kælr í froste.

> Constraint gives scant choice;
> a naked man is chilled by the frost.

Icelandic rune poem:

> Nauð er Þýjar þrá
> ok þungr kostr
> ok vássamlig verk.
> opera niflungr.

> Constraint
> grief of the bond-maid
> and state of oppression
> and toilsome work.

Modern rune poem by E. Vongvisith:

> In the cold autumn woods
> there is no dry, there is
> only weather and wet,
> and the need for warmth.

> Two sticks, found under
> a rock, dry—but can they
> make what is needed to
> keep us alive for the night?

> We find the heat in friction,
> in patience, persistence,
> and at last, joy of joys,
> the tinder sparks alive.
>
> My arms ache, splinters
> crust my hands, but
> the fire now crackles
> in defiance of the rain.

Impressions of the rune

Through personal experience, I associate Sigyn very strongly with this rune. Sigynn usually comes to me in a very whimsical and childlike fashion, but Nauthiz connects me to Sigynn in Her darker aspects—Sigynn as She holds the bowl over Loki's face, capturing the poisonous venom and filling His most desperate need. It is a rune of desperation, often of desperate courage. It is also rune of tight binding; it locks down wild energy. There is much emotion associated with this binding rune. It can help one carry on despite emotional turmoil, pain, and upset. I have used it to bind extremely anxiety-ridden people and to soothe them, upon their request.

I also see a hidden aspect to this rune: "needfire"—the dark, often painful burning need or hunger of the soul to be filled with (and to fill) the Gods. In many ways, Nauthiz is a rune of endurance in the face of emotional shattering. It is that desire, hunger, and determination so potent that one endures and continues going forward even when the outcome is uncertain. This makes it an extremely important rune spiritually, for it will help us piece ourselves together and persevere when all our facades have been stripped away. Nauthiz contains all those things that temper our spirit and help us grow strong and resilient. That is the secret of this rune, its resiliency. It is the fire in which a hand-forged blade is annealed: it tempers, strengthens, and creates a thing of unique, unparalleled quality out of the rawest of materials. We all need (no pun intended) a little Nauthiz in our lives or we will fold in the first heavy gale of challenge.

This is also a rune of loyalty, of holding the course despite trouble, difficulties, and inconveniences. It is the friend who stands by you when your world is crumbling, whose quiet support helps you steady yourself and pull through. It is a rune of endurance and survival. Pain, anguish, conflagration are all taken within, tempering and strengthening the soul and character. It gives depth and quiet power to the spirit. Because of this, Nauthiz is necessary for a healthy spirit. It is what enables us to transform the experiences we have, and what makes us capable of establishing a good name and doing good works. It gives lasting power. It is the precious *odhr* and *hamingja* (personal power and luck) that is passed from mother to child, the sinew that lies hidden within our ancestral bonds. It represents the difficulties and challenges that force us to surpass ourselves.

Nauthiz is not a rune of aloneness. Its very nature implies that one needs to be involved with something external to oneself. Spiritually, it brings you to the realization that, at times, you will find yourself in situations greater than all the things that the Gods have put within you. Those are the times that you have to go to the Gods directly, to seek outside help to pull through. Looking at the rune metaphorically as fire tool, you are one stick, the power and energy of the Gods is another stick, and rubbed together, they provide the fire necessary to help you survive. Everyone has their own personal Nauthiz, their own needfire. Every person in a "Nauthiz situation" must discover what steps he or she must take to overcome that situation. It's a personal rune in that its solutions are different for each person. That said, you can recognize and appreciate when other people have gone through this rune, which can be a bonding experience. This bonding through great struggle has the potential to create kindred spirits, true friendships, and great trust between people.

For most of us, the most difficult challenges are those that have to do with spirituality. Nauthiz infuses that into your friendships. Your own spirituality will flow easily in the presence of those who have also internalized this rune. Fire was utterly essential to our Ancestors for surival. In a way, fire is our eldest Ancestor and, as such, it connects us to the very first humans who huddled around a bonfire, terrified of the dark. That necessity permeates every aspect of this rune. Indeed, necessity itself is part and parcel of this rune's nature. It is the spark of warmth and heat that allows life to bloom.

God(s)/Goddess(es) I associate with this rune:
   Sigyn.

Miscellaneous associations:
   fire, fire tools (flint, tinder, fire-bow), obsidian, jet, lava stone, needfire, need, constraint, binding, carefulness and precision with a task, steadfastness, the pain and anguish of deepest need.

Isa

Traditional meaning: ice

Anglo-Saxon name: Is

Phonetic equivalent: \i\

Anglo-Saxon rune poem:
   Is byþ ofereald, ungemetum slidor,
   glisnaþ glæshluttur gimmum gelicust,
   flor forste geworuht, fæger ansyne.

   Ice is very cold and immeasurably slippery;
   it glistens as clear as glass and most like to gems;
   it is a floor wrought by the frost, fair to look upon.

Norwegian rune poem:

> Ís kollum brú bræiða;
> blindan þarf at læiða.

> Ice we call the broad bridge;
> the blind man must be led.

Icelandic rune poem:

> Íss er árbörkr
> ok unnar þak
> ok feigra manna fár
> glacies jöfurr.

> Ice
> bark of rivers
> and roof of the wave
> and destruction of the doomed.

Modern rune poem by E. Vongvisith:

> The whole thing—
> waiting for the icicle to drop
> and spear the crust of snow,
> that poised anticipation
> some call stasis and others
> have named entropy,
> that ceaseless "now"—
> that's what you must seek,
> that everlasting moment.

Impressions of the rune

Isa is a rune of stillness and quiet, of going into oneself to find that place of quiet contemplation so necessary for spiritual growth. It is a centeredness, but one that is ever-ready to tap into wildly kinetic, crackling, Jotun-born energies of synergy, transformation, and change. I see Skadhi particularly with this rune because it is the silence of the hunter, and because it resonates with the cold, wild music of the icy tundra. I also see northern lights and a deserted snowy landscape of firs and wolves and cold.

I have often used this rune to cast a diamond-hard, reflective personal shield. There is a glittering quality to Isa; I often see it as a sheet of hard ice capturing and repelling the stark winter sunlight. It is containment, centering, and stillness, but it isn't without movement. It is like the limb of a tree: hard, unyielding, and plain, yet deep within surges a river of life-giving sap. Isa is far more than what it appears to be on the surface. Its beauty is not that of the delicate flower but rather, the starkness of a finely tempered blade. It is implacable, unyielding, unswerving. It allows nothing to impede its progress. Isa is the place of quite contemplation—not passive, but bursting with life and potential. It is the nurturing solitude wherein all creativity is born. It's the roiling life-filled darkness beneath the polar ice, seemingly still and contained from the outside but really incredibly vital and kinetic on in the inside. There's an electric quality to this rune.

Isa is a rune of boundaries. Too often in our interactions with other people (especially in love relationships) we give too much of ourselves; we scatter ourselves. Isa prevents this. It guards our necessary personal boundaries. It guards against soul loss. In this, it works very well with Mannaz, which teaches healthy, balanced communication and partnership, and with Ior, which is all about setting and maintaining healthy boundaries, as well. Isa teaches us how to cherish the self, not to the exclusion of other relationships but as a necessary core component of them. Isa is that place within the self that must be protected, nurtured, and cherished at all costs.

Because of that, it is can be a rune of intensely dynamic interaction. You must be very confident in yourself to interact with someone who is firmly grounded in Isa. In its negative aspect, Isa can take that self-protection to negative and unhealthy extremes, making you reclusive and cold. It is a warrior's rune, the rune of one who has found the source of his or her self-hood and power and has leapt into it, claimed it, and is using it judiciously but with full conscious intent.

Isa is like a foundational post that supports a dwelling. It can also be like a nithling pole, because both of these things are symbols of protection and power. There is a special integrity to Isa. Water is transformative: It can be steam, running water, still water, or ice, yet its chemical composition does not change. Within that is a mystery.

God/dess I associate with this rune:
   Skadhi.

Miscellaneous associations:
   ice, winter, Herkimer diamonds, diamonds, white calcite, clear quartz, shielding, warding, centering, self-containment, arrows, spears, walls, fir, wolves.

Jera

Traditional Mmaning: harvest
Anglo-Saxon name: Ger
Phonetic equivalent: \j\, \y\

Anglo-Saxon rune poem

   Ger byÞ gumena hiht, ðonne God læteþ,
   halig heofones cyning, hrusan syllan
   beorhte bleda beornum ond ðearfum.

   Summer is a joy to men, when God, the holy King of Heaven,
   suffers the earth to bring forth shining fruits
   for rich and poor alike.[11]

Norwegian rune poem:
   Ár er gumna góðe;
   get ek at o,rr var Fróðe.

Plenty is a boon to men;
I say that Frothi was generous.[12]

Icelandic rune poem:

Ár er gumna góði
ok gott sumar
algróinn akr.
annus allvaldr.

Plenty
boon to men
and good summer
and thriving crops.

Modern rune poem by E. Vongvisith:

The wheel turns
as the sod crunches
frozen beneath the cart.

The wheel turns
as the snow melts
and the plow bites
into the earth's darkness.

The wheel turns
as the rains come
and light green dusts
the breast of the field.

The wheel turns
and golden stalks wave
in warm, lush winds
under a brilliant sky

The wheel turns
as the scythe whooshes
through the golden stalks
at the time of harvest.

The wheel turns
and time repays you
for the patience you've shown
about the seeds you sowed.

Impressions of the rune

Jera is a keeper of time, a gentle swaying of tone, texture, and timbre of the Wyrd-web. It can conjure images of Yggdrasil and its leaves, often in vibrant autumnal colors. This rune can open doors for passages between states of being and between the worlds. Sometimes it manifests as the web itself, stretching amongst the boughs of the Tree. In this guise, everything can be tracked and read though it. It is also a shuttle used to weave the web.

Jera has strong connections with planting and seasons and harvesting, embodying the well-known quote from Ecclesiastes: "To everything there is a season."[13] It is a rune of gentle, slow maturation, and also of seeds drinking in strength and vitality while lying hidden in rich, dark soil. This is a transformative rune, a rune of flexibility and growth; it ever so gently teaches one to expand one's boundaries and incorporate new learning and concepts. It teaches one to gently expand one's limits, reaching them ever onward and outward. Spiritually, it is that neutral ground where we meet the Gods halfway, that tentative place of courtship where we find ourselves edging ever slowly toward greater openness to the Gods.

I often see Loki with this rune. In one of the Eddic tales, Loki hides from the other Gods and, as He is hiding, weaves the first fishing net (later He tries to escape by turning into a fish and is captured in the very net He invented). When His presence is evident with this rune, I've seen Jera as a net, which can be used to capture incoming energies. This leads me to concur that not only can this rune be cast as a very unique ward—a net to capture and /or repel unwanted energy—but it may also be a useful tool in soul retrieval. Jera can sew up old emotional and spiritual wounds. It teaches us to "process" these wounds and glean wisdom from our experiences. In fact, I would say it is a rune of careful maturation of the spirit. I study *iaido* (Japanese sword work) which is a very disciplined and precise art. It can take years to truly develop skill and style. In one of my classes, one of the senior students was talking about the process of training and how it might best be approached. He said, "It cannot be forced, only molded." And that, I think, is the essence of Jera. It is that process of molding.

There is a definite rhythm to this rune, but it is deeply contained. Jera is patient crafting and waiting—not passively, but with practice and hard work, and with the knowledge that brilliance will come. It is a rune of slow, measured growth, often hard-won and all the more precious for it. It represents the slow evolution of our spirits throughout the entire soul-span of our Wyrd throughout our lives. It's that patient building that keeps us moving toward the Gods. With Frey, that rhythm can come with the insistent drum beat of life pulsating in the earth, of the seeds pushing up to the sun—a deep, primal, insistent, pounding rhythm.

Jera is about cycles on all levels. It is about growth and reminds us that there is wisdom to be gotten from every cycle we have gone or will go through. It's actively taking advantage of every step along the way of a cycle, not just quietly going through it. It's organic and is influenced by its environment. This rune is dependent upon its environment for its evolution and its behavior, just as nature is. It's like a plow: It only works if you push it. Jera cannot make you go through a cycle. You have to work for it. It's up to you to take as much from it as is needed for you to complete the cycle. It's not a "pushing" rune. It's nothing like a cattle prod.

Jera can also represent the life/death cycle. It can be helpful in guiding a dying person to the realm of the Ancestors as long as they're not fighting the process, kicking and screaming. In its simplest aspect, Jera is the wheel of time, the turning of the seasons, the slow balance of an ecosystem. It is the cycle of light and darkness, yin and yang, day and night. In this way, it may be associated with the house of Mundilfari, the Gods of the cosmological cycles, especially Mani, the Moon God, and Sunna, the Sun Goddess. This is particularly true when it is combined with the rune Dagaz.

God(s)/Goddess(es) I associate with this rune:
    Frey, Loki, Nornir, Idunna, Mani, Sunna, Erda.

Miscellaneous associations:
    spiders, webs, the web stretching around Yggdrasil, the
    weaving of the web, passage of seasons, time, fishing nets,
    yellow, orange, russet, amber color, autumn, autumn
    leaves, seeds, salmon, clay, ochre, yellow topaz.

Eihwaz

Traditional meaning: yew
Anglo-Saxon name: Eoh
Phonetic equivalent: \e\

Anglo-Saxon rune poem:
    Eoh byþ utan unsmeþe treow,
    heard hrusan fæst, hyrde fyres,
    wyrtrumun underwreþyd, wyn on eþle.

    The yew is a tree with rough bark,
    hard and fast in the earth, supported by its roots,
    a guardian of flame and a joy upon an estate.

There are no Icelandic or Norwegian rune poems for Eihwaz.

Modern rune poem by E. Vongvisith:

> Stand strong, you
> solid-built one, heavy
> with burdens, hardened
> with labors, stand strong.

> Your home and family
> lie behind you, safe,
> protected, all you hold
> dearest and best-loved
> guarded by your hands
> moving a staff

> back and forth, twirling
> like the wheel of the seasons
> you ride to till and sow,
> harvest and store, like
> the birth of children
> and the death of old ones.

> Stand strong, freeman,
> and let none pass, for you
> protect all that which gives
> you life, sustenance, breath.

Impressions of the rune

Eihwaz is a gateway rune. It is Yggdrasil itself—a source of power, reservoir of energy, a gateway to journeying. As a manifestation of Yggdrasil, it is harnessed power. This rune is not as explosively kinetic as Isa. It is a flowing, contained reservoir of power, but it expands. Where Isa crackles, the power of Eihwaz flows. One might say that it is contained fire, a slow burn to Isa's ice. Whereas Isa's power gives one the ability to act without, Eihwaz gives the ability to journey and act within. They balance one another.

It is particularly appropriate that this rune means "yew." Opinions vary as to whether Yggdrasil is an ash tree or a yew tree. Some rune-workers believe that it contains part of every tree, while others believe that it changes depending on who is seeking it out. Regardless, the yew is a very powerful tree. Amongst the ancient Celts, it was a favored tree for making bows. It is extremely poisonous and has strong associations with death. Magically, the power of yew can be used to remove the toxic effects of the abuse of power and knowledge, or taking misguided shortcuts to power. It brings both truth and humility in its wake. It is a tree of learning, but there is an element of sacrifice in its nature. The spirit of yew teaches that hubris is poison. It teaches us that the true adept never ceases to seek humility. It has the power to show one the truth about oneself. In this way, it is ultimately a tree of healing. Its secondary lesson is that every ending is a beginning and that stagnation, too, is poison. All of this is contained with Eihwaz, as well.

This is a very difficult rune to plumb. Eihwaz teaches the organic component of things. In magic you have energy reservoirs, and it's necessary to recognize the organic nature of those reservoirs. Basically, trees just don't grow by themselves. They have to get nutrients from somewhere. It's the same with magical systems. We often go into magic assuming that the energy will just be there, but Eihwaz teaches that these things are organic: you have to give back and nurture yourself and the reservoirs you're drawing from. One can't always just take without giving anything back in return. Eihwaz is about using resources wisely, including our own inner resources. You have to take care of yourself to be sure you can keep going without getting overloaded. In the mundane world, this rune can teach a powerful work-life balance, which can carry over into shamanic work and seidhr, too. Wherever you find your source of power, there will come a time when you have to take care of it, feed it, and nurture it. Every time you seek it out, Eihwaz will show you a different part of the Tree. Every time there is a different reason, a different meaning for you in what parts of the Tree you are meeting. Each place that Eihwaz/Yggdrasil takes you will tell you something about yourself and how your psyche and spirit are working. This rune connects everything and every world. There's a tension in this rune—a rough, rasping tautness—whether it's Odin on the Tree, suspended before the true anguish began, or the whisper of danger that so often heralds a Deity's presence, I do not know. Both? Neither? It can be a very grim rune.

God(s)/Goddess(es) I associate with this rune:
    Odin.

Miscellaneous associations:
    earth, fire, yew, Yggdrasil, axis mundi, eagle.

Perthro
Traditional meaning: a device for casting lots[14]
Anglo-Saxon name: Peorth

Phonetic equivalent: \p\

Anglo-Saxon rune poem:

Peorð byþ symble plega and hlehter
wlancum [on middum], ðar wigan sittaþ
on beorsele bliþe ætsomne.

Peorth is a source of recreation and
amusement to the great,
where warriors sit blithely together in the
banqueting-hall.

There are no Icelandic or Norwegian rune poems for Perthro.

Modern rune poem by E. Vongvisith:

You will confine yourself
to destiny, like a child
made to stay inside
on a hot, fair day.

You will become a leaf
floating along the rain flowing
in the gutters, down the drains.

You'll dance your luck
under a roof of stars,
or spear it
among water-lilies,
or feel each grain of it
slip through your fingers.

What you will not do
is forget:
the dice cup rattles
and the game changes course
all the time.

Impressions of the rune

Perthro is a visionary rune. It represents the well of Urd, which contains all that was, all that is, and all that will be. All possibilities, memories, and potentialities rest, inchoate and unformed, within this rune. It is the primal sea, the primal womb from which every creative work, idea, magical endeavor, and spiritual epiphany can be plucked. There is immense wisdom in this rune. It is a passageway between states of being, including the cycle from birth to death to rebirth. Perthro allows one to look beyond the temporal, beyond the obvious, beyond the physical, for what might lie beneath. Although it is not a healing rune per se, I do occasionally find a connection to Eir in that can be used to evoke prophetic or insightful dreams, including healing dreams that restore the mind, body, emotions, and spirit.

A difficult rune to interpret, Perthro envelops like a chrysalis. At the same time, it contains the potential for vision, inspiration, wisdom, and knowledge to burst forth in a flood.

Because it is connected to Urda's well, Perthro is transformative. It peers down into the primal void of Ginnungagap; to plumb its depths is to reach into the very chasm of creative and destructive power. It contains the raw material from which the threads of Wyrd are crafted. It's appropriate that this rune falls right in the middle of the Futhark. In this light, I occasionally see Frigga plucking from Perthro that which She spins upon Her spindle. (Some modern devotees of Frigga have divined through personal gnosis that She spins the threads that the Nornir later weave into Wyrd.) This rune holds in nascent form all the potential being-ness of creation. It also holds those parts of ourselves that we have lost or locked away. It is a well of memory. It provides a map of all that we have been, all that we are, and, most importantly, all that we can be.

There is something about this rune that has a lot to do with Ancestors. It is also connected to Mimir's Well. Odin plucked out his eye as a sacrifice of exchange in order to drink a single draught from Mimir's Well. The wisdom within Perthro almost forces the seeker to sacrifice. However, the sacrifice is not an eye or any other body part; rather, it is the search for self-awareness. It is the moment when we "find ourselves," truly find our center, both accepting and acknowledging who and what we are. In some odd way, Perthro contains its own self-sacrifice because you realize where you are and what your place is, and that the future is based on what you do. With this very knowledge it forces you to go down different roads and make different choices, because you cannot do anything else and still be true to the added wisdom that you have gained from this rune. Gifts don't always have to be as dramatic as plucking out an eye to be powerful. When you look into the Well, it may not seem a sacrifice at all, but a self-evident necessity.

I do not associate Perthro with daily contemplation. You must really prepare to plumb this rune. It's very undefined on its own. This rune is like a mirror in that if no one is looking into it, what is there to reflect? It needs someone to stand gazing into it in order to come alive. How you are the moment you decide to go into this rune determines what you see and get out of it. Because we are always changing according to our choices and experiences, the possibilities contained within this rune for each person are endless. Perthro, too, constantly changes. Therefore, the juncture at which you decide to visit it is key.

Perthro can come up in a divinatory reading to indicate that there is no way to tell at the moment of the reading what the outcome of the situation being read will be. It may be that one is not ready to know for one reason or another, or, more often, that no particular course of action is standing out, Wyrd-wise, more than any other. The future really isn't set.

God(s)/Goddess(s) I associate with this rune: Nornir, Eir, Frigga, Mimir.

Miscellaneous associations: Datura, water, Well of Urd, womb, birth, death, passages, awakening, mugwort, labyrinths, cups, dice.

Algiz

Traditional meaning: Elk

Anglo-Saxon Name: Eolh

Phonetic equivalent: \z\

Anglo-Saxon rune poem:

> Eolh-secg eard hæfþ oftust on fenne
> wexeð on wature, wundaþ grimme,
> blode breneð beorna gehwylcne
> ðe him ænigne onfeng gedeþ.

> The Eolh-sedge is mostly to be found in a marsh;
> it grows in the water and makes a ghastly wound,
> covering with blood every warrior who
> touches it.

There are no Icelandic or Norwegian poems for Algiz.

Modern rune poem by E. Vongvisith:

> He stands, guardian
> of the bridge, knight
> who defends it
> with life and honor.
>
> See his hand come out
> to challenge you, and
> think on whether or not
> what he asks is yours
>
> to fight, or to refuse,
> and whether the struggle
> is worth what lies, near or far,
> at the other side of the bridge.

Impressions of the rune

Algiz is a powerful rune of protection. It makes an excellent warding rune for a home; when cast as a shield in this manner, it may appear as boughs of Yggdrasil, interwoven into a dense wall impossible to penetrate. I associated it with ash trees, with Yggdrasil, and with the strength of the Valkyries. This rune is a shield. Algiz contains the strength of Yggdrasil, that part of Yggdrasil that supports the web and all the worlds. It is dense yet very focused. Occasionally, I see Odin's spear, Gungnir, with this rune. Algiz contains within itself the ability to both nurture and protect. In addition to its use as a shield, it is also a healing rune and can add strength and help heal injuries. It is very useful in grounding, both on an emotional and a physical level. It has the potential to knit together that which is broken or damaged.

On an esoteric level, Algiz is the staff that brings the will of the magician to bear directly on the mortal plane. It is focused will—watchful, decisive, and unswerving, with all the carefully contained force of a hurricane. Though it is wood and not air, it connects to Ansuz in this way. Rather than cleanse by sweeping through, it protects against that which would corrupt and harm by sweeping away. Algiz is a solid, stable, and very firm rune. It makes a good fence or wall, and functions nicely to guard one's Wyrd and one's property. When it comes up in a reading, it may be a sign of protection and blessing. Its protective nature makes it a very positive rune. Reversed, it might indicate a need for protection, an excessive scattering of one's attention and energies, being too sponge-like, not standing up for oneself, or being drained of energy. In this way, I see it as enclosing sacred space. Unlike Kenaz, it isn't the process or means of hallowing, but it marks what has already been hallowed.

I associate Algiz with strength of the spirit and a firm, sturdy character. However, it's not a wall so hard and rigid that nothing affects it; it not completely impenetrable. Algiz asks, "Can you stand your ground even against the threat of penetration?" It's not solid like Isa. It is strength of spirit in the face of daunting challenge and attack. That strength of spirit doesn't come from yourself, as it does with the other runes. There is something about this rune that connects to the blessing of the Gods, to the Ancestors, to your kin and kindred as sources of strength and courage. It is this network of connections on the physical and spiritual levels that helps to render one impenetrable to attack. Like the great World-Tree, Yggdrasil, Algiz connects all worlds, all roads, everything. Part of what Algiz can teach is knowing not only what or who you have standing behind you, but what you yourself also bring to that link. It is this that gives strength. When I first started working with Algiz, I would often see groups of Valkyries in my meditations. It is worth noting that I never saw it with just one Valkyrie, but rather, always with a group. You have to acknowledge and link into the sources of your strength. This rune teaches you how to be part of a working whole.

In upright position, Algiz can be used to indicate birth, and in its reversed position, death.

God(s)/Goddess(s) I associate with this rune:
Valkyries, Odin, Freya.

Miscellaneous associations:
ash tree, spears, the boughs of Yggdrasil, wood, petrified wood, iron, steel, squirrels, agates, birds of prey.

Sowelo

Traditional meaning: sun
Anglo-Saxon name: Sigel
Phonetic equivalent: \s\

Anglo-Saxon rune poem:

Sigel semannum symble biþ on hihte,
ðonne hi hine feriaþ ofer fisces beþ,
oþ hi brimhengest bringeþ to lande.

The sun is ever a joy in the hopes of seafarers when they journey away over the fishes' bath, until the courser of the deep bears them to land.

Norwegian rune poem:

Sól er landa ljóme;
lúti ek helgum dóme.

Sun is the light of the world;
I bow to the divine decree.

Icelandic rune poem:

Sól er skýja skjöldr
ok skínandi röðull
ok ísa aldrtregi.
rota siklingr.

Sun
shield of the clouds
and shining ray
and destroyer of ice.

Modern rune poem by E. Vongvisith:

Above us, the sun, radiant
in Sunna's chariot, rides
and carries this day forward
into the memories of the old
and the hopeful hearts of the young.
Victory is as warm as rays
from the oldest fire we know,
joy as tangible as the heat
rises from the earth herself.

Impressions of the rune

This rune is a cataclysm, a lightening-quick burst of spiritual awakening. It is an opening, a sudden rush of inspiration and insight. It is energy of the sun, warm and filled with vitality. It breaks through intellectual or metaphysical darkness the way a beam of sunlight suddenly pierces dark storm clouds. It has the contained, focused force of a bolt of lightening striking the ground. Indeed, I often see lightening shattering an oak tree when I meditate on this rune. I find that it often comes up in readings to indicate an impending surprise, often a challenging one. I occasionally associate this rune with Loki.

I see the power of the sun with Sowelo, a power that also crackles and dances. It's an enthusiastic rune. It helps one make one's mark on the world, both physically and spiritually. Sowelo is a rune of attainment. It is a warm rune, a rune of restorative vitality. I often use it in combination with Uruz and Berkana for overall healings. It restores the energy and the spirit.

Sowelo is also a rune of blessings. A great deal of spiritual rejuvenation can come out of Sowelo. It is a victory rune, and can be used to remove the obstacles and dreck in one's path. It is a rune of daring, of chutzpah, of cunning, of taking the initiative and creating the circumstances one wants. It is an intensely active rune; it strikes and opens. It can be violent in that striking, engaging in offensive action, but not with the emotion of Thurisaz. Sowelo is strong and flamboyant but not vicious. It can also indicate radical and often unpleasant and unexpected change. For this reason I tend to interpret it somewhat negatively. For me, it's the destruction of the lightening strike.

Sowelo is connected to the sun from which we derive heat and nourishment. In the Northern Tradition, the Sun Goddess is named Sunna. She is mentioned in the Second Merseburg charm, a 10th-century charm from Merseburg, Germany, as possessing the power of healing.[15] Ancient peoples who relied extensively on agriculture for their survival would surely have revered the healing, nourishing power of the sun. One of the ideas contained within Sowelo is that just as the sun provides us with physical nurturing, so the Gods will provide us with spiritual nurturing that we need. This is a very comforting idea, just as some people find comfort in the warmth and beauty of the sun itself. Sowelo reminds us that we can have that same joy of being in relationship with the Gods and Ancestors. In living our lives, and in honoring our Gods and the dead, we should ideally experience that same rejuvenation that we automatically receive when the sun rises each day. Along with clarity, that appreciation for the flow of things is part of what Sowelo can bring.

God(s)/Goddess(es) I associate with this rune:
    Loki, Sol/Sunna, Farbauti.

Miscellaneous associations:
    fire, lightening, dandelions, goldstone, the sun, sunstone, narcissus oil, frankincense, bees, citrine, lightening-struck wood

The Third Aett

The third aett is, to my mind, the most complex of the entire Futhark. Whereas the first aett is all about inspiration and motivation, and the second is about endurance and perseverance in the face of necessity, the third aett moves beyond these two binaries. With this aett, there is a sense of "the magician triumphant." It speaks of the ability to manifest one's will while balancing one's gifts with necessary humility. There is a healthy tension amongst these runes, and a sense of their power being equally woven between Midgard and the other worlds. The runes in this aett speak to power made manifest, skills acquired and balanced by hard-won wisdom. More than any other aett, these runes take one beyond the individual experience into the realm of connectivity, communal synergy, and reciprocal social bonds.

Tiewaz

Traditional meaning: Tyr
Anglo-Saxon name: Tyr
Phonetic equivalent: \t\

Anglo-Saxon rune poem:

> Tir biþ tacna sum, healdeð trywa wel
> wiþ æþelingas; a biþ on færylde
> ofer nihta genipu, næfre swiceþ.

> Tiw is a guiding star; well does it keep faith
> with princes;
> it is ever on its course over the mists of night
> and never fails.

Norwegian rune poem:

> Týr er æinendr ása;
> opt værðr smiðr blása.

Tyr is a one-handed god;
often has the smith to blow.

Icelandic rune poem:

Týr er einhendr áss
ok ulfs leifar
ok hofa hilmir.

Týr god with one hand
and leavings of the wolf
and prince of temples.

Modern rune poem by E. Vongvisith:

Are you the one
who will stand up, speak openly,
lift your hand and
plunge into battle?
Are you prepared to absorb
the cost of the fight?
Are you the armored one
who waits in impatience
for the horn's call?

Receive the challenge,
answer the summons,
witness the injustice, and
open to the pleas of others,
for you are the spear, the sword,
the fiery speech, the pen,
the rifle, all that yearns
for the just battle
fought to the bitter end.

Impressions of the rune

This is the rune of the individual warrior. It is a rune of discipline, courage, perseverance, self-reliance, and duty done despite hardships. It is also a rune of mental clarity. As Tyr does, this rune guards against moral relativism. It is staunch and unwavering, strong in belief and practice. It is a rune of character, ethics, and, yes, morality. It is doing the right thing, "walking your talk" and not bending from what is right no matter what the circumstances, even when it may cost you your personal honor and reputation. The rune is named specifically after the God Tyr. Tyr is one of the Aesir, and is often associated with warriorship and justice. He sacrificed his sword hand to ensure the binding of the great wolf of chaos, Fenris. Fenris is one of the sons of Loki and the giantess Angurboda. It is prophesied in Norse cosmology that, one day, Fenris will break free of all constraint and destroy Odin at Ragnarok. The Gods were gravely concerned as They watched Fenris grow and decided that something had to be done, for the wolf grew stronger every day. They sent to the Duergar in Svartalfheim, a race of beings known for their immense skill at crafting, and commissioned a rope made of six impossible things: the spittle of a bird, the beard of a woman, the footfall of a cat, the nerves of a bear, the roots of a mountain, and the breath of a fish. The Duergar crafted a cord that was rich in magic and impossible to break, yet thin and supple as a silken ribbon. The Gods then sought out Fenris and enticed him into a test of strength, binding him first with heavy ropes, then chains, and then stronger bonds. Each time, the wolf broke his bonds without any effort. Finally the Gods brought out the ribbon. Fenris suspected a trick and only agreed to test the enchanted ribbon if one of the Gods would place His sword hand in the great wolf's jaws as a pledge of trustworthiness. Knowing what would occur, Tyr did so. When the wolf could not break the ribbon, and when the Aesir refused to free Him, He closed His jaws and bit off Tyr's hand. The interplay of honor and betrayal, sacrifice and duty underlying the story of Tyr and Fenris is integral to understanding Tiewaz. The antithesis of this rune is a person of malleable character who changes sides and beliefs depending on who is around. It is a rune of cold, steel-bright clarity.

This is a fierce rune, but cold and incredibly disciplined. It rises above the sway of emotions and has a certain focused detachment about it. It is a cold fire that burns within, a driving force that cuts through all the crap. In many ways, this rune is the outward, higher manifestation of the same energies that drive Isa. But Tiewaz is in no way a contemplative rune. It is a rune of right decisive action. There is an intense focus to this rune; indeed, it is almost frightening in its intensity. When I meditate on Tiewaz at work, all the little details that I might otherwise have missed snap into sharp, clear focus.

The warriorship that Tiewaz represents is beyond the constraints of gender. It can be equally present in men or women. That said, I have occasionally seen Tiewaz come up in rune readings to indicate virility and/or male sexuality. I have also seen Tiewaz come up reversed in rune spreads to indicate someone of poor, untrustworthy character, or to indicate a need to step back and reconnect with one's priorities. It can also indicate a run-down, battered spirit in need of reconnecting with its power.

Tiewaz is all about being able and willing to do what is right despite painful consequences. Whereas the runes before Tiewaz are either energy or the manipulation of energy, Tiewaz is all about self-regulation and self-mastery, about seeing how well you've internalized the lessons of the other runes and how effectively you use those lessons learned for manifestation in Midgard. It's a test rune in that it determines how well you've mastered the lessons of all preceding runes. It's necessary to let Tiewaz go where it wants to go.

This rune also teaches some fundamental things about warriorship. One should not get caught up in the trappings of what it means to be a warrior, or in one's identity as "warrior" or, conversely, "not a warrior." Everyone can benefit from Tiewaz; everyone has the capacity to find some aspect of warriorship within themselves. Tiewaz can be a key to that process. Tiewaz keeps you honest. It's a rune of stark, unbending integrity. I connect it with giving and keeping one's word. This rune is like the *bushido* code of the samurai or the concept of *giri*, those wrenching times when duty and desire conflict and duty gains the upper hand. This rune can also help the shaman, spirit-worker, or seidrh-worker snap back into linear time/reality if he or she tends to have difficulties while engaged in trance-work or journey-work.

God(s)/Goddess(es) I associate with this rune:

Tyr.

Miscellaneous associations:

justice and any symbols of justice, warriorship, weapons, steel, swords, tiger's eye, solomon's seal, spikenard.

Berkana

Traditional meaning: birch
Anglo-Saxon name: Beorc
Phonetic Value: \b\

Anglo-Saxon rune poem:

> Beorc byþ bleda leas, bereþ efne swa ðeah
> tanas butan tudder, biþ on telgum wlitig,
> heah on helme hrysted fægere,
> geloden leafum, lyfte getenge.

> The birch bears no fruit; yet without seed it
> brings forth suckers,
> for it is generated from its leaves.
> Splendid are its branches and gloriously adorned
> its lofty crown which reaches to the skies.

Norwegian rune poem:

> Bjarkan er laufgrønstr líma;
> Loki bar flærða tíma.

> Birch has the greenest leaves of any shrub;
> Loki was fortunate in his deceit.

Icelandic rune poem:

> Bjarkan er laufgat lim
> ok lítit tré
> ok ungsamligr viðr.
> abies buðlungr.

> Birch leafy twig
> and little tree
> and fresh young shrub.
> Silver fir, protector.[16]

Modern rune poem by E. Vongvisith:

> Full of life, abundant, bursting
> seed and floods of milk, I
> revel in rich soil, create life,
> nourish it, alive, fecundity
> unrestrained, bones and blood blooming
> hot and moist beneath lush skin,
> breasts overflowing, belly heaped
> like a haystack, fingers curling over
> stems of fresh flowers opening
> wantonly to the sun's caress,
> my hair rippling green in the wind,
> a sea of tallgrass, or golden as pampas,
> or dark like the tangled vines of the forest floor.

> Or I, the war-hammer's keeper
> in peacetime, frith-weaver who bears
> a knife within my skirts, a bear
> who mercilessly defends my cubs,
> the wildcat's piercing scream unheeded
> as I spring to shield my babes,
> shudder of thunder ignored while I,
> with terrible gentleness, carry each one
> through the dark night, rain and howling,
> from one riverbank to the other.

Impressions of the rune

This rune is gentle yet firm. It soothes and encourages and gently mends that which is broken. Its traditional association is the birch, which is a fascinating tree in its own right. Birch is a "colonizing tree," which means that its presence creates favorable conditions for other trees to grow. After a piece of land has been ravaged by fire, birch is often the first tree to come back. It has multiple medicinal uses, and its bark is highly astringent.

Magically, birch heralds a time of new beginnings and new opportunities. It is also highly cleansing, both energetically and physically. (Bundles of birch branches are often used as part of the cleansing process of a traditional sauna.) It can be used to get one's energy flowing, and its cleansing properties are fairly gentle. On an occult level, the energies of this tree are very helpful in handling change on all levels. It's particularly effective in integrating changes to one's energy-body. There is a connection between this rune and *frith*, or peacekeeping. It can be used to create a favorable atmosphere in which to work. I often see pale blues, soothing grays, and silvers when I work with this rune.

I often associate Frigga with this rune, as Her presence brings with it a quiet firmness. She will coax, but always without impeding one's own strength or growth. Berkana is a rune of growth and healing. It contains the strength of the mountain, the restorative power of bubbling clay pools, the agility of a bird in flight, and the subtle staying power of ancient trees. It contains, as Frigga does, rock-solid strength and far-seeing wisdom. Perhaps because I associate Berkana so strongly with Frigga, it reads as a very feminine, almost motherly rune to me. According to some sources, the ancient Rus worshipped the birch tree as a Goddess in her own right.

Berkana lends one the ability to reach down into the endless storehouse of ancestral power, specifically through the

Disir, and draw up the wisdom and strength one needs for healing. It connects the lifeline of the past to that of the present. It helps create a solid foundation—not overly influenced by emotion yet definitely compassionate, and oriented toward upward growth and evolution. It is this connection with hidden ancestral energies that most connects it to Eir and other healing Goddesses.

At its root, Berkana deals with the birthing process. This is a *conscious* birthing, meaning that it is about choosing exactly what it is you're going to manifest out of a particular process, because it is necessary to continue the threads that your Ancestors have already woven. Whether or not it actually comes down to giving birth to a child, it's the process of realizing that whatever you manifest affects the whole Wyrd-thread, the line that you came from, and everything else you manifest in the future. So Berkana cautions you to choose wisely. It teaches the responsibility of upholding a legacy, the values and principles that have been instilled and passed down through generations and generation.

Berkana teaches the naturalness of this process of spiritual growth and all the ways that can manifest. It isn't a cold rune. It has a sense of joy and pride, especially the pride of being a part of this process. This pride also means that whatever you manifest, you should be able to be proud to show it to the Deities you worship and your kin. Once Berkana manifests, you should feel spiritually proud of the works you do with it.

Berkana is a rune of foundation. It also teaches you to be aware and to really look for those manifestations of your lineage out in the world. With Berkana I think of wood, and how the grain has its own language. The whole earth has its own language and endless patterns, as well. Everywhere we go, there are layers and layers of experience and history. Berkana is being aware of the struggles and spiritual awakenings of the past and really looking with the eye of the spirit to connect all these levels of history to who you and where you are now. It makes you aware that just because cities topple and kings and queens fall, it doesn't end the manifestations of those eras and people. In this way, Berkana is a rune of living history. It is a rune of foundation. It connects.

Berkana is fulfilling and life-giving on all levels. It gently recharges with the resonance of Jera. It's not violent. It can also remove you, ever so slightly, from a great wounding or pain within so that you can begin the process of abrading and healing. It makes things grow. (This last comment was added by my 5-year-old goddaughter who was so happy to have gotten something so right that it was included in my notes. She is, however, exactly correct: Berkana does, indeed, make things grow.)

Because it is a rune of frith-weaving, it is a particularly good rune for blessing children or a household.

God(s)/Goddess(es) I associate with this rune:
    Frigga, Holda, Jord, Eir. I know several people who see
    Sigyn with this rune, as well.

Miscellaneous associations:
    birch, the birthing process, growth, healing (especially
    heart-healing), nurturing, compassion, acceptance of
    passages, light blue, geese, Fensalir, cattails, aqua aura
    crystals, seeds, lilies, mugwort, comfrey, red clover,
    goldenseal, blue apatite.

Ehwaz
Traditional meaning: horse
Anglo-Saxon name: Eoh
Phonetic equivalent: \ē\

Anglo-Saxon rune poem:

> Eh byþ for eorlum æþelinga wyn,
> hors hofum wlanc, ðær him hæleþ ymb[e]
> welege on wicgum wrixlaþ spræce
> and biþ unstyllum æfre frofur.

> The horse is a joy to princes in the presence
> of warriors.
> A steed in the pride of its hoofs,
> when rich men on horseback bandy words
> about it;
> and it is ever a source of comfort to the restless.

There are no Icelandic or Norwegian poems for Ehwaz.

Modern rune poem by E. Vongvisith:

> Strong and patient,
> the horse plods on.

> His back is sturdy
> and his hooves solid.

> The road passes by
> steadily under his feet.

> His head is high as
> he fixes his gaze

> on the horizon which
> is coming ever nearer;

> slowly but patiently
> the strong horse plods on.

Impressions of the rune

Ehwaz reminds me of Sleipnir because it is primarily a rune of journeying, especially between the worlds. It opens doors and heralds movement forward from one situation to another, better situation. Ehwaz calls to mind Yggdrasil as Odin's steed; as such, Ehwaz has the potential to be our "steed" as we journey between the worlds. There is also a connection between this rune and possessory work. Although this practice remains controversial within the Heathen community, Deity possession (wherein the presence of a God or Goddess pushes aside a person's consciousness and acts and speaks directly through that person), it is being embraced with increasing frequency. Many who incorporate this practice into their work utilize Afro-Caribbean terminology, calling the person who is being possessed a "horse," with the God or Goddess as the "rider" and the person as the one being "ridden." Ehwaz can represent that relationship of the possessing Deity to the receptive "horse." (This topic is a bit beyond the scope of this book, so I encourage interested readers to seek out *Drawing Down the Spirits* by Raven Kaldera and Kenaz Filan for more information.)

This rune tends to be very image-intensive. It can represent the shimmering, liquid rainbow bridge that flows between all the worlds, although it's less the bridge than it is the journey itself as one traverses it. It is here that I often see a connection with Gna, who is a messenger Goddess and one of Frigga's retinue. Ehwaz has something of Her energy and presence. Ultimately, Ehwaz is a rune of communication. It helps one communicate on the temporal plane as well as with one's allies, totems, Ancestors, and Gods/Goddesses.

Because of its associations with journeying, it is easy to see Odin as Gangleri the Wanderer with this rune. Ehwaz is a messenger rune; it gets through and around every blockage. There's also something about this rune that can open doors and reveal passages and pathways. I find it appropriate that "Eihwaz" and "Ehwaz" sound so much alike. One is the steed of Odin and the other can be our steed through the worlds.

Ehwaz often comes up in readings to indicate rapid change, a need for change, or the presence of the Gods. Reversed, it can indicate blockages and a lack of necessary flow.

God(s)/Goddess(es) I associate with this rune:
Odin, Gna, Sleipnir.

Miscellaneous associations:
comfrey, horsehair, horses, midnight blue, grey, old-fashioned travel cases for letters, stamps, messages and the delivering of messages.

Mannaz

Traditional meaning: man

Anglo-Saxon name: Man

Phonetic equivalent: \m\

Anglo-Saxon rune poem:

Man byþ on myrgþe his magan leof:
sceal þeah anra gehwylc oðrum swican,
forðum drihten wyle dome sine
þæt earme flæsc eorþan betæcan.

The joyous man is dear to his kinsmen;
yet every man is doomed to fail his fellow,
since the Lord by his decree will commit the
vile carrion to the earth.

Norwegian rune poem:

Maðr er moldar auki;
mikil er græip á hauki.

Man is an augmentation of the dust;
great is the claw of the hawk.

Icelandic rune poem:

Maðr er manns gaman
ok moldar auki
ok skipa skreytir.
homo mildingr.

Man
delight of man
and augmentation of the earth
and adorner of ships.

Modern rune poem by E. Vongvisith:

I am in your house.
I am in your village.
I am in your country.
I am your family.
I am your tribe.
I am your nation.

Blood does not link you.
Genes do not link you.

I am the bonds of frith.
I am friendship and fellowship.

Blood alone does not bind you.
Ancestry alone does not bind you.
Only your heart forges the tie.
Only your hands cement the tie.
I am the oath spoken and unspoken.

Impressions of the rune

Stephen Pollington notes that this rune may be linked to a divine Ancestor named Mannus, first mentioned by Tacitus in *Germania*.[17] Certainly, as the wisdom of this rune unfolds, it speaks to work and partnership and the reciprocity of social interaction. Mannaz is a rune of balanced partnership. It is an equal give-and-take, a healthy flow of energy in which no one is giving too much or too little. To some extent, it teaches healthy social boundaries. Where Isa is introspective and concerned more with the self, Mannaz is concerned with maintaining healthy boundaries with others. For this reason, I connect it strongly to Gerda, the wife of the God Frey. Gerda's name means "enclosure," and, like Skadhi, Gerda can help teach one to maintain a healthy independence. She can teach one to effectively guard one's boundaries, even in the midst of effective social interaction.

Mannaz is essentially comprised of two Wunjo runes facing each other. This opposition calls to mind relationships, be they be friendships, working relationships, or romances. Often this rune comes up to indicate romantic attachments and/or marriage. One of its lessons is not giving too much of oneself in a relationship and maintaining ones' independence so that the relationship continues to be two wholes coming together, not two halves making one whole. There is a sense of self-containment and self-awareness, and even confidence, in this rune. It cautions strongly against the type of soul-loss too often seen in unhealthy romantic relationships, in which one person sacrifices everything and loses him- or herself in the other. The poet Khalil Gibran wrote about love and partnership in a way that beautifully reflects the lessons of this rune:

> "...let there be spaces in your togetherness,
> And let the winds of the heavens dance
> between you.
>
> Love one another, but make not a bond of
> love:
> Let it rather be a moving sea between the
> shores of your souls.
> Fill each other's cup but drink not from one cup.
> Give one another of your bread but eat not
> from the same loaf
> Sing and dance together and be joyous, but let
> each one of you be alone,
> Even as the strings of a lute are alone though
> they quiver with the same music."[18]

Mannaz helps keep relationships vital and healthy. This rune will not make sense until you have developed a strong sense of self in your relationships. Mannaz can be anything; it reflects what is within you, but also what is in your partner. In that dance there should be equal tension, equal synergy. This rune tells you that you can't let your need to be with someone override what it is that is vital to your soul.

Mannaz makes one look beyond appearances. It teaches one to judge the value of love itself separately from the value of the love relationship. The love in a particular relationship may be good, but the relationship itself may not be good for you at all. There are other criteria for the making of a strong relationship besides the existence of love. Sometimes love is not enough. The two vertical staves in each Wunjo teach that both people have to be firmly rooted in something. For instance, one person can't be deeply spiritual and serious about his or her job while the other has no spiritual beliefs and isn't serious about anything. Both have to be firmly grounded for it to work. Mannaz also touches on how much difference you are capable of tolerating within a relationship. In this, it is a rune of healthy compromise (or healthy lack of compromise, as the case may be).

On a different level, this rune does have certain wealth connotations but that is not its main augury.

God(s)/Goddess(s) I associate with this rune:
 Gerda, Frey, Njord.

Miscellaneous associations:
 rose thorns, silver beauty roses, garnets, brown,
 icy lavender, rings (especially wedding and
 engagement rings), brown agate, blue quartz, clasped
 hands (in affection or in the traditional business
 handshake).

Laguz

Traditional meaning: water

Anglo-Saxon name: Lagu

Phonetic Value: \l\

Anglo-Saxon rune poem:

> Lagu byþ leodum langsum geþuht,
> gif hi sculun neþan on nacan tealtum
> and hi sæyþa swyþe bregaþ
> and se brimhengest bridles ne gym[eð].

> The ocean seems interminable to men,
> if they venture on the rolling bark
> and the waves of the sea terrify them
> and the courser of the deep heed not its
> bridle.

Norwegian rune poem:

> Logr er, fællr ór fjalle
> foss; en gull ero nosser.

> A waterfall is a River which falls from a
> mountain-side;
> but ornaments are of gold.

Icelandic rune poem:

> Lögr er vellanda vatn
> ok viðr ketill
> ok glömmungr grund.
> lacus lofðungr.

> Water
> eddying stream
> and broad geyser
> and land of the fish.

Modern rune poem by E. Vongvisith:

> I see you far above
> cresting the cliff's sharp boundary,
> patience that wears away even rock
> with the menacing roar coming
> from unseen rapids ahead.
>
> Drop by drop, you progress
> in a mighty tide, rush down
> mountainsides in trickling herds,
> growing stronger by gravity's pull,
> finally racing along river channels
> to spend yourself in a great gasping sigh
> at the wet delta where two kinds of water meet.
>
> You are all
> about the flow
> of one thing
> into the other.
>
> And so I see you also
> in the cracked, dry lines of city streets
> where I walk every day,
> in scrawled spray-painted totems
> and the lines in newspapers—
> in the days and nights I pass in and out of,
> and in my dreams too,
> signs and symbols to be read with the heart,
> showing me the way in which
> to let myself flow,
> to be carried over the cliff's edge
> into the frothing, joyous chaos at its foot.

Impressions of the rune

Laguz is water, but can also manifest as liquid fire, roiling lava, or moving heat. This rune encompasses all the ways we consciously use energy, power, and attraction. There is an intensely sexual element to this rune. If one engages with its power in no other way, it can easily be reached during the give-and-take of sex. This is an intensely magical rune. At its deepest levels, it deals with responsibility, and the effect one's consciousness and mental and emotional state has when one is working magic. There is an element of the shape-shifter to this rune because water, by its very nature, transforms itself. Water must be contained, but it takes the shape of its container. Laguz is like that and thus can be very deceiving. It is very easy to dismiss the power of this rune when one is contemplating a mere bowl of water, but it's not so easy to do so when one is standing before the Atlantic or Pacific ocean listening to the crashing song of the waves as they roll in. The potentiality of Laguz exists in both the bowl and the ocean. Laguz flows and spirals and surges beneath the surface of everything and takes whatever form you choose. It is a rune of the manifestation of desire.

Many runes provide raw energy and a source of power, but Laguz teaches the rune-worker how to make the flow of that energy work for him- or herself. Laguz teaches the rune-worker how to manipulate energy to the best effect. Many of the runes are themselves energy sources, but Laguz teaches how that energy flows, how it feels when it flows, and how to actively manipulate it and work it.

Laguz is one of the easiest runes to use to change your awareness (for example, from temporal reality to the other-worlds). This is an intensely kinetic rune, too; it can make you look for that same energy thrill in other runes. This is when it's possible to really go into each rune and internalize its energies. When that happens, the rune-worker no longer stands at a distance from the rune. With Laguz you can't be aloof; you can't just look at it as you would watch a river flow by. Laguz is a river you want to dive into, swim in, and work from its center.

Laguz flows in a very distinct manner. River water can only flow in a certain direction because of gravity and topography, but not so with this rune. Laguz can travel anywhere because it is full of life energy. Because of this, the rune-worker can take from it and simultaneously be replenished by it. Instead of being drained after working Laguz, one can actually feel better and more energize. Because there is such an element of deception and glamour about this rune, it is an excellent rune to use to bend people to your will. It is subtle and seductive and will make anything you suggest seem reasonable. It would be the perfect rune to use to feed a magical illusion. This rune creates links between people through which energy/hamingja can be passed. In many ways, it is a rune of hamingja directly applied and manifested. For those who do journey-work, this rune is particularly useful in changing or camouflaging one's otherworldly appearance.

When Laguz is used in healing, it can manifest as a needle used for stitching up a wound. It allows the body's energies to flow uninterrupted. (Author's note: I am not suggesting that rune magic should take the place proper medical care. However, I see nothing wrong with using one's runic skills to augment traditional healing methodologies.)

This is a very changeable rune. It can bring to you what you desire but it does so by flowing into every possible opening and subtly shifting things in your favor. It's the velvet glove hiding the iron fist, so to speak, for although it does not have a hard feel at all, it can overcome, overpower, and burn. It is the power of the ocean at its wildest. It is the power of the tides and the ocean deep. This is what this rune is made from and what it taps directly into.

God(s)/Goddess(es) I associate with this rune:
    Ran, the Nine Daughters of Ran, Gullveig, Freya
    (particularly as Mardoll), Loki.

Miscellaneous associations:
    flow, desire, sexual attraction, amber, gold, sex magic,
    damiana, goldschläger, good alcohol, mead, oceans.

Inguz

Traditional meaning: Ing (the God Frey)

Anglo-Saxon name: Ing

Phonetic Value: \ng\

Anglo-Saxon rune poem:

> Ing wæs ærest mid East-Denum
> gesewen secgun, oþ he siððan est
> ofer wæg gewat; wæn æfter ran;
> ðus Heardingas ðone hæle nemdun.

> Ing was first seen by men among the East-Danes,
> 'till, followed by his chariot,
> he departed eastward over the waves.
> So the Heardingas named the hero.

There are no Icelandic or Norwegian poems for Inguz.

Modern rune poem by E. Vongvisith:

> He comes, fair in form,
> fair in face, radiant as light
> given shape and body, arms
> bare, tattooed wrists alive
> with sheaves of grain,
> hair golden like waves of it,
> streaming in the late summer run.

> He comes, and the wailing goes up
> as the sickle flashes, as the crone
> draws bright blood from Him,
> and His bride weeps, veiled
> like the shadow that forms
> sharp, in the brightest light.

> His descent is the same every time,
> but every time is meaningful.
> Take note, you who are asked
> to give and give, and not stop
> until you have given all.

Impressions of the rune

There is a quality about this rune that speaks very strongly of a doorway. It has to do with completion. Inguz is not so much a doorway to descent or to the "great beyond"; rather, it is a comforting doorway—a marker door, a familiar door, a way home. This rune represents completion, not through something that is unknown but, rather, through something you may have forgotten or something that was there all along and which you may have just realized or discovered. It is a rune of quiet revelation and discovery. All of those things you subconsciously hide from yourself and all of those areas you have to work on for healing and growth are contained in Inguz. It's an advanced rune; it keeps the Shaman, seer, spirit-worker, and mystic sane and healthy. It's not a rune for the beginner. It's not meant to be. You have to know the area you are exploring in order to find Inguz there. Inguz is what you use—the doorway or the system—that advances you from one stage to the other in astral work and shamanic work. It's a rune of gentle opening.

In its crudest aspect Inguz can represent the vulva, which, of course, mirrors the symbology of a doorway. Inguz has an organic nature to it. More than just a doorway, it's whatever you bring across that threshold and whatever you choose to take back. It's also what happens when you cross through, discover what you need, and take something (knowledge, wisdom, experience) back to where you were before. It's that entire cycle.

It is also the castrated, slaughtered God whose blood feeds the land. This is the sacrifice of self and the attendant rebirth. Here Inguz speaks of Frey as Lord of the Fields and God of the Harvest, the John Barleycorn whose yearly sacrifice makes the fields fertile. There's learning and growth and improvement here. You learn and discover something every time you go through Inguz, and you must use that knowledge wherever you can in your daily life. Inguz is about fertility and ever-renewing growth. It's about sacrifice of the self to further that growth, yet it is not a violent rune. This rune, which in its very shape echoes Jera, speaks to the cyclical turning of the seasons, the cosmological cycles, and the inevitability of change.

There is a purity to Inguz. It can be very good for warding and protecting children. Magically, it can be used to keep out negative energy. This rune has a gentle light that dispel darkness and reflects serenity and calmness. Inguz can be a healing rune, and as such, it reflects serenity and calmness. It's also a rune of beauty in that it can bring out a person's inner beauty, instilling them with quiet self-confidence. Although it lacks the deceptive qualities of Laguz, is also a very good rune to use in casting a glamour. It can be cast with a certain mirror-like, reflective quality that can then be infused with whatever message one wishes to convey.

Inguz is a reflective rune for women. A woman working with Inguz will eventually be required to examine how she values herself as a woman and the ways in which she wastes her power, especially sexually. Conversely, a man may find himself called to examine his ideas and expression of masculinity. Inguz will also occasionally come up as an indicator of pregnancy in a reading. As a healing rune, Inguz is an excellent rune to meditate on for inner-child work and it can bring emotional and spiritual renewal. Of course, it is a birthing rune—not so much giving birth to a child, but giving birth to the blossoming of one's own spirit.

Inguz is a visionary rune, good for scrying and as a cue for astral journeying. It contains all the impetus for growth that Frey as God of the fields can bring, yet it does so without pushing or force. Rather, it beckons at a more sedate pace. It is a rune of grace, not just spiritual grace but pure physical grace of movement. For this reason, martial artists and dancers may find it useful to meditate on this rune before practice.

It is power evenly balanced and distributed. It is beauty, but not shallow physical beauty. Rather, it is the beauty of a soul perfectly balanced and moving forward into growth and spiritual evolution.

God(s)/Goddess(es) I associate with this rune:
Frey, Idunna.

Miscellaneous associations:
reflections, warding, scrying, calmness, mirrors, sexuality, innocence, water, lightalfheim, doorways to other worlds, white, rainbow moonstone, white calcite, yarrow, elder berry, sacrifice.

 ## Dagaz
Traditional meaning: day
Anglo-Saxon name: Daeg
Phonetic equivalent: \d\

Anglo-Saxon rune poem:

Dæg byþ drihtnes sond, deore mannum,
mære metodes leoht, myrgþ and tohiht
eadgum and earmum, eallum brice.

Day, the glorious light of the Creator, is sent
by the Lord;
it is beloved of men, a source of hope and
happiness to rich and poor,
and of service to all.

There are no Icelandic or Norwegian poems for Dagaz.

Modern rune poem by E. Vongvisith:

Turnaround,
heads-up—
the bottom of the bottle
throws you out
with gleeful force—
sunlight comes in
through dirty windows
to light up the dim room.

The end of the wait
becomes final—
the last of the night
disappears, never to return.
You get up out of bed,
tired and sad no longer
and run downstairs.

And everything now seems
the color of violets
or the sky burnished
by the break of day.

Impressions of the rune

Dagaz is first and foremost a rune of transformation, whether it be the transformation of night into day, or season into season, or a life-shattering change in one's circumstances. Dagaz often comes up in rune readings to indicate a serious internal, spiritual transition in one's life. It is a powerful rune; the reader will often find that the other runes thrown in a reading will in some way revolve around Dagaz.

Magically, Dagaz can be cast to reveal the truth of a situation or to turn a situation to one's own advantage without drawing undo attention to oneself. Because it is connected to the cosmological and natural cycles (the calendar, the clock, the seasons), it creates a macrocosm in which the microcosm of one's magical work can be concealed. This rune pulls no punches, however; if it comes up in a rune-reading heralding transformation, it's important to be aware that such transformation can be brutally life- altering. Although it is not always a comfortable rune, it is usually positive, even when it indicates rapidly shifting change. When it comes up in a reading in this capacity, I often connect it very strongly to Loki.

Dagaz can indicate a dynamic union of opposites, the synergy of complementary forces working effectively together. In this way it can reflect the wisdom and power of the Moon God, Mani, and Sun Goddess, Sunna, who govern the transition of day into night and vice versa. One of the lessons Dagaz teaches is that things are always in flux, and the only constant is change. This can be a powerful message and lifeline when one's circumstances are particularly difficult. Dagaz also teaches us to find the doorway, the means, and the opportunity for changing our circumstances. It can make them readily visible even in the midst of personal chaos.

Focusing on the exact middle of this rune is an excellent meditation tool for trance-work and astral journeying.

God(s)/Goddess(es) I associated with this rune:
  Loki, Mani, Sunna.

Miscellaneous associations:
  transformation, dreaming, journeying, Ostara, the sun, the moon, calendars, clocks, hourglasses.

Othala or Othila

Traditional meaning: inherited wealth, homeland, family estate.[19]

Anglo-Saxon name: Oethel

Phonetic Value: \ō\

Anglo-Saxon rune poem:

> Eþel byþ oferleof æghwylcum men,
> gif he mot ðær rihtes and gerysena on
> brucan on bolde bleadum oftast.

> An estate is very dear to every man,
> if he can enjoy there in his house
> whatever is right and proper in constant
> prosperity.

There are no Icelandic or Norwegian poems for Othala.

Modern rune poem by E. Vongvisith:

> This is what you've been
> working and paying for,
> this place of comfort, wealth
> embedded in the fields,
> walking about on hooves
> solid or cloven. This is
> your family's seat, your
> wife's hearth, your children's
> inheritance. This is home,
> and you are a part of it,
> here until you die, and then
> part of it still, your name
> whispered or sung aloud,
> your wealth spent, remade,
> your children's children
> pausing to drip honey mead
> on the barrow-mound which
> shields your dead body as you
> shielded this place in life.

Impressions of the rune

Othala represents one's home, both literally and figuratively. It stands for everything over which one has right of ownership. It is the continuity of one's ancestral line, the wealth and inheritance one receives from one's Ancestors. This is inheritance on every possible level—not just money or land, but genetics and all that implies, as well. Like a link in a never-ending chain, it is our connection to all those who came before us and all those who will come after us. At its most basic level, it is *odal land*, one's ancestral land. It may also stand for one's homeland as well as those of one's Ancestors. It is the connection to one's ground. It is all the strength, power, luck, and protection that one has a right to by birth and blood. Othala can also represent the hall of the Ancestors, as well as their ongoing protection and blessing.

This is a powerfully protective and defensive rune. It makes an excellent protective rune to cast over one's home and threshold. It can function this way precisely because Othala represents the concept of lawful ownership. It is what belongs to you by right and thus represents what you yourself have the right to protect and guard. As such, this rune is all about boundaries and territory. In this case, however, it isn't personal boundaries, but the boundaries of one's property. Where does one end and the other begin? What is truly yours? What do you own? Where does your sphere of influence end? Where are your roots? Whence do you draw your greatest strength and nourishment? These questions are all inherent in Othala.

Othala is a good rune to use when embarking on ancestral work for the first time. It springs from that preexisting connection to one's forefathers and -mothers. It can help one become more aware of that connection. If, when honoring one's Ancestors, there is difficulty in feeling that connection, Othala can help. It embodies the ongoing process of exploring one's genealogy and then applying that to Ancestral veneration. It is the transition of power and wealth from one generation to the next. This rune makes a good esoteric boundary marker around one's property and personal territory.

Othala is often connected to Odin in His role of sacred king. In this respect it is a rune of sovereignty, but be warned: It implies not just entitlement, but responsibility, as well.

When Othala comes up in a rune spread, it is a very positive sign of stability and protection. Reversed, it indicates a need to reevaluate one's actions and priorities and reconnect with the source of one's strength.

God(s)/Goddess(es) I associate with Othala:
Odin, Hella.

Miscellaneous associations:
shielding, Hlidskjalf (Odin's throne), granite, basalt, Ancestors, soil, coins, one's house, wealth, genealogy.

Learning the Runes

The first exercise should be done before you ever open a book on runes, and it then should be repeated after the runes are learned. Actually, it's not a bad idea to repeat it from time to time over the course of your study, as the results can be enlightening.

Exercise 1

Choose a rune. Center yourself, clearing your mind of all outside influences. As you gaze at the rune, take note of any images, thoughts, feelings, smells, or sounds that come to mind. Spend about 10 minutes on the rune and write down everything that comes to you. Go as deeply into the image of the rune as you can. In time, this will comprise your own personal notebook of runic correspondences. At times, when gazing into a rune, it is possible to enter into a deep trance and actually access the Wyrd realms through the image of the rune.

Exercise 2

After the first exercise has been completed, it is time to begin galdr. It is of utmost importance to enter into this with no preconceived expectations regarding the runes. They will reveal themselves during the course of the galdr, often in unexpected ways and very seldom exactly the same way twice.

For this exercise, center and ground. Choose a rune and visualize its image forming in front of you. If your sight isn't particularly strong, feel it forming there. Begin to chant, starting with its name. This may feel a little silly at first, but eventually the rune will guide the chanting. The point of this chanting isn't to sound pretty or elegant. As you chant, allow images, thoughts, and feelings to form in your mind and work those images into the chant. Galdr can be done through chanting, singing, intoning, and even *joiking*; it's a combination of all of those things and more. Let the rune guide you. Basically, sing what you see, always returning to the rune name when the images falter. After 10 or 15 minutes of this, ground the energy. (Were this an actual magical casting, that energy would be sent along the Wyrd-web, which every good rune-worker eventually learns to see, read, and manipulate.) Ground yourself and write down everything you remember about the experience. If you actually managed to access the web-worlds, your eyes may feel a bit odd and unfocused. This is normal. Vision can take a bit of time to readjust to the physical world. Please be aware that the runes will not reveal themselves in their entirety, even after years of study. It is an ongoing journey, a process of probing the endless faceted depths of each and every rune. Give it time, and practice without fear and with full concentration. It should be noted that rune casting can become a very kinetic experience.

Exercise 3

The third exercise is to write a poem for each rune. All of these things will help the novice develop an understanding of and a personal relationship with the runes. There are three extant sets of rune poems. They are very much analogous to the word knots, or kennings, given for each Ogham. They are the keys to interpreting certain aspects of the runes and thus bear great study. I've provided the English translation for each poem. Each one provides a specific key for understanding a specific rune. I also encourage readers who are interested in an historical examination of each rune to look at the texts listed in the bibliography. Having an historical context for the rune poems and for the linguistic development of the runes themselves can be very helpful in understanding the way they interact with Midgard.

4 The Anglo-Saxon Futhorc

Most rune-workers I know work exclusively with the Elder Futhark, the 24 runes described in the previous chapter. Recently, however, there has been a growing interest in the extra Futhorc runes, the Anglo-Saxon and Northumbrian runes not included in the original Futhark. Raven Kaldera, one of the first people to write about using these runes as a Northern Tradition Shaman, notes: "As I studied them…I was moved and shaken by the deep meanings of the extra runes. They are dark, complex, and difficult; their concepts are ambivalent, and they reek of the Rokkr or Jotnar, the 'dark gods' of Norse mythology."

For this reason, they may not be everyone's proverbial cup of tea. For those rune-workers interested in incorporating these runes into their practice, I feel it's important to cover their meanings here. I tend to stick to the Elder Futhark because it is what I first learned and began to use. There is no reason why these "extra" runes can't be added to one's kit, however. I know many people who read with the combined Futhark and Futhorc runes. Although many modern Heathens and Norse Pagans associate them with the Jotnar

Deities, those associations are not historical, but rather, stem from the personal gnosis of modern practitioners.

(Many thanks to Raven Kaldera for allowing me to quote from his article on the Futhorc runes. The original article may be located on the Northern Shamanism Website: *http://www.northernshamanism.org/Futhork_Runes.html.*)

Ear—Rune of the Grave

Traditional meaning: hanging tree, grave, earth

Phonetic equivalent: \ea\

Anglo-Saxon rune poem:

> Ear byþ egle eorla gehwylcun,
> ðonn[e] fæstlice flæsc onginneþ,
> hraw colian, hrusan ceosan
> blac to gebeddan; bleda gedreosaþ,
> wynna gewitaþ, wera geswicaþ.

> The grave is horrible to every knight,
> when the corpse quickly begins to cool
> and is laid in the bosom of the dark earth.
> Prosperity declines, happiness passes away
> and covenants are broken.

There are no Icelandic or Norwegian poems for Ear.

Modern rune poem by E. Vongvisith:

> The singletree sways
> in the wind, awaiting
> the rider, the newly dead,
> the swine or kine
> whose life is spent
> and whose body is meat
> for the larder of peasant,
> thrall, lord or king.

She stands still
at the end of the road,
awaiting the wanderer,
the newly dead, king
or lord, thrall or peasant,
whose life is spent
and whose body rots
within the burial mound.

Fame may burn brightly
for centuries, but the body
takes time to return to
that from which it was made.

Impressions of the rune
Raven Kaldera:

"It is sacred to Hel, the Lady of Death whose home is open to all, who is half beautiful woman and half rotting corpse. The rune itself is shaped like a singletree, the hanging yoke that a newly slaughtered animal is hung on upside down for ease of butchering. As I live on a farm and butcher my own livestock, the single tree strikes a strong chord in me. It reminds me of all that dies so that I and my family, tribe, and community may live.

Such is Ear's message. Like the Death card in the Tarot, Ear speaks of how death and loss are part of the cycle of life. In order that one thing may live, another must die. We cannot subsist on anything that was not once alive. Even the vegetables that we eat grew out of other rotting vegetation. Life gives way to death which brings life again. The Rune of the Grave reminds us that everything passes, all is impermanence, but that each loss will usher in a new part of the story...and that this cycle is the only thing that is permanent, that can absolutely be counted on. Hel's power is absolute, and it is eternally unchanging even as she brings eternal change to our lives.

Ear generally means that your life, or some part of your life, needs a total reboot. It's not about whether or not you should do it—there is a definite element of nonconsensuality to Hel's rune. Ear says that it *will* happen, because it's time and because it needs to happen. How painful it is depends on your attitude. The only thing that you can control, in the end, is how you will meet the oncoming onslaught.

The internal death spoken of by Ear, however, is not a fast and furious death. It is the long slow rotting down of gradual but inevitable change. That means that this rune can be used for galdr purposes to do that, and it's particularly good for letting-go spells. I've given it as a talisman to people who were divorcing and needed to learn to live whole different lives over the next few years."

———————

This is a rune of transitions, of passage from one state of being into another. It may present itself in a reading to herald a time of dissolution, change, movement, or spiritual challenge. It is a rune of rot and decay, and it teaches us that these things are part of the natural, organic cycles of life, and that they are occasionally necessary in our spiritual lives, as well. Ear appears to tell us that it's time to let go and move on.

God(s)/dess(e)s I associate with this rune:
    Hella.

Miscellaneous associations:
    soil, stones, bones, rope, petrified wood, dia de los muertos figures.

Ac—Rune of the Oak Tree

Traditional Meaning: oak

Phonetic equivalent: æ

Anglo-Saxon rune poem:

> Ac byþ on eorþan elda bearnum
> flæsces fodor, fereþ gelome
> ofer ganotes bæþ; garsecg fandaþ
> hwæþer ac hæbbe æþele treowe.

> The oak fattens the flesh of pigs for the
> children of men.
> Often it traverses the gannet's bath,
> and the ocean proves whether the oak keeps faith
> in honourable fashion.

There are no Icelandic or Norwegian poems for Ac.

Modern rune poem by E. Vongvisith:

> Strong is the oak which stands
> firm in the earth, deep roots
> shooting down, down
> into the dark loam, past topsoil,
> past clay, into the stratus
> of crumbling rock.

> Water drinking in through rootlets
> that lead to roots that feed
> the mighty trunk, swaying
> with its leafy green crown
> in the gentle winds of spring,

> or tossing its head in gales
> that whip branch and leaf
> harshly to the ground, yet
> the trunk stays firm, rooted
> in what it knows to be real.

Only time and age may work
their slow magic of decline
on this tree, this survivor,
quiescent and yet tougher
than even the depredations
of storm and drought. See,
and take heart, you who
would seek this for your own.

Impressions of the rune
Raven Kaldera:

"The glyph for this rune is that of a person holding a stick. Although there's no lorebound basis for it, the entity who seems to speak up for this rune whenever I use it is Angrboda, the Hag of the Iron Wood, first wife of Loki. Oak was one of the trees referred to as "iron wood" because of its strength and endurance, and also because it was frequently struck by lightning and exploded in fire. Thor (and other storm deities) has a close association with oak trees as well. This is largely due to a natural coincidence: due to its rough bark and specific cellular makeup, oak trees are poor conductors and the lightning tends to blow them up rather than run smoothly down them. Because of this, they are revered for bringing controllable fire to humanity.

The figure of Angrboda is that of a female Jotun, or giant; she is seen as tall, immensely strong, and very assertive. She also brings forth powerful children— Fenris, the great wolf who nearly ate the world; the Midgard Serpent that surrounds it, and Hel, the Goddess of Death. Unfortunately, she was secretly killed by Odin, who feared that she and Loki would populate the entire world with such creatures and thus overthrow his regime. It is said that all Loki found of her was her ashen heart, burnt like the heartwood of an oak tree.

To draw the rune Ac is to be the lightning rod for the fears and anger of others, whether or not it is deserved. You will have to stand as strong as the oak tree, and endure the blows and flames. If it does not kill you, it will make you stronger. Ac's keyword is Endurance, as opposed to the other 'strength' rune, Uruz/Ur. Ac is the rooted tree and the high mountain. Indeed, there is something very 'masculine' about Ur's strength, that of the wild charging buffalo, while there something more feminine (but not passive) about Ac's strength. Consider one the irresistible force and the other the immovable object.

I use Ac for healing galdr, as I also use Ur, and a bind rune of the two is especially good to put on someone's body (with bodily fluids, or Sharpie if you don't have that kind of relationship) in places that need strength and endurance. I put that bind rune on my knees when I have to hike, as mine are in pretty bad shape."

Ac is a rune of stoic endurance. It is the embodiment of perseverance in the face of impending storm, great obstacles, or emotional travail. This is the rune that says, "I may bend, but I will never, ever break." It is the staff that one can lean upon, and the truncheon with which one may guard oneself or one's territory. This is a rune of strength. When I work this rune, I often see the strength of a mountain that simply cannot and will not be moved by any storm that passes over it. I see eagles flying, circling high above the tree tops. I see roots, thick, fat, and ancient, digging so deeply into the soil for so many generations that they cannot be dislodged. I see the strength of stone, of earth, and of the quiet fury that says, "I will not yield, ever." Ac is a good rune to call upon when one needs to persevere in a difficult task or during a particularly challenging time of personal struggles. It is an excellent ally when a job needs to be done and one's strength and will is fast fading.

God(s)/Goddess(es) I associate with Ac:
   Thor, Angurboda.

Miscellaneous associations:
   staves, oak, lightening-struck wood, oak leaves, acorns.

Ior—Rune of the Serpent

Traditional meaning: unknown. (Pollington postulates that it might be an amphibious creature akin to an otter.[1] Many modern Northern Traditionalists associate it with Jormungand, the World-Serpent.)

Phonetic equivalent: io

Anglo-Saxon rune poem:

   Iar byþ eafix and ðeah a bruceþ
   fodres on foldan, hafaþ fægerne eard
   wætre beworpen, ðær he wynnum leofaþ.

   Iar is a river fish and yet it always feeds on land;
   it has a fair abode encompassed by water,
   where it lives in happiness.

There are no Norwegian or Icelandic poems for Ior.

Modern rune poem by E. Vongvisith:

   The great Snake undulates
   through the waves, water
   rushing in cascades off

its shiny, scaled back,
motion after motion,
leading it onward, forever
circling the boundaries
of Midgard. Far out to sea,
the Serpent circles,
holding, protecting, letting
no one and nothing pass
but also keeping us inside.
A circle is both shield
and enclosure, a boundary
has two sides, like a coin,
like the Snake, like the sky.

Impressions of the rune
Raven Kaldera:

"This is clearly dedicated to yet another of Angrboda's children, Iormundgand the Midgard Serpent, the largest snake in the world whose coils surround the entirety of Midgard. Iormundgand is also the boundary between Midgard and everywhere else, and this is the secret of this rune. Its lower-octave keyword is Boundaries, and getting it in a reading may mean that you need to set boundaries for yourself. (I use it in galdr as a good boundary-setting rune for this purpose, often in bind-rune form with Eihwaz for defense or Algiz for protection, and I've given it as a talisman to codependent people who need to form better boundaries.) It's higher-octave meaning is the reminder that every boundary is actually liminal space, and to stand there is to be a part of both things.

Unlike Fenris who is clearly male and Hel who is clearly female, there is some confusion over Iormundgand's gender. Some see him as male, others see her as female. Serpents are very hard to sex, and they are associated throughout history with gender-ambiguous deities—Shiva, Dionysus, Ariadne, Athena, Lilith—and with regeneration, and wisdom. Iormundgand's gender is as slippery as hir [sic] scales. I've noticed that men seem to sense him as male, and women sense her as female, so personally I think that s/he falls into that third category of Neither And Both.

Yet, as cosmic hermaphrodite, s/he surrounds everything, making a boundary around the whole world. To be both male and female is a powerful place, because you take in everything. As one gender-crossing individual stated, "I'm just like everybody else…only more so." To surround everything, you must bring opposites together, because opposites divide and thus are antithetical to Iormundgand's job.

Thesis-antithesis. Black-white. Male-female. To extract one's self form this constant war or opposing forces, you must drop out of the war entirely and come to a new place, a point called Synthesis. At this point, you realize that you actually have both poles within you, and you stop embracing one and demonizing (and projecting) the other. To draw Ior is to stop putting yourself on one side of the ideological camp, and finding yourself in both places, and thus surrounding the entire issue. Only when you can see it from every perspective can you accurately figure out what to do."

———

Ior is a Northumbrian rune. It is a rune of boundaries, of knowing when to maintain them and when it is healthy and right to yield. It may indicate the need to strengthen one's boundaries or be more vigilant in general. This is especially so when this rune appears reversed, in which case it indicates that the querent has very poor, unhealthy boundaries, indeed. Ior might appear to indicate the need for greater fluidity of thought, approach, or action. This rune is like a serpent in that it can slither and slide into every hidden corner, every unmarked crevasse. Ior challenges assumptions and dispenses with the neat little mental boxes and categories that we seem to love so much. Ior also has the capacity to ferret out hidden secrets, fears, phobias, and anxieties. This is the serpent that churns up the waters of our subconscious whether we want him to or not.

Ior can also be used to ward and protect, marking boundary points and blocking off an area for protection. I find it particularly good for warding windows and mirrors. Meditating on this rune can be very helpful in learning to navigate the emotional side of relationships, particularly in determining what issues and emotions are yours by right to own and which are not your responsibility. Ior is all about owning one's emotions and taking responsibility for oneself. It can teach you how not to get lost in someone else's emotional chaos. It can also teach you to stand your ground without aggression and with quiet, innate confidence.

God(s)/Goddess(es) I associate with this rune:
> Jormungand.

Miscellaneous associations:
> snakes, snakeskin, reflective surfaces (mirrors, glass),
> multi-colored glass, water.

Yr—Rune of the Archer
Traditional Meaning: yew bow
Phonetic equivalent: y or ü

Anglo-Saxon rune poem:

> Yr byþ æþelinga and eorla gehwæs
> wyn and wyrþmynd, byþ on wicge fæger,
> fæstlic on færelde, fyrdgeatewa sum.

> Yr is a source of joy and honour to every
> prince and knight;
> it looks well on a horse and is a reliable
> equipment for a journey.

Norwegian rune poem:

> Ýr er vetrgrønstr viða;
> vænt er, er brennr, at sviða

> Yew is the greenest of trees in winter;
> it is wont to crackle when it burns.

Icelandic rune poem:

> Ýr er bendr bogi
> ok brotgjarnt járn
> ok fífu fárbauti.
> arcus ynglingr.

> Yew
> bent bow
> and brittle iron
> and giant of the arrow.

Modern rune poem by E. Vongvisith:

> The drawn and cocked arrow
> points far away.

> Tension in the wrist,
> keen eye, poised
> for the right moment.

> Taut bowstring and
> the archer's stillness
> like a thunderclap of nothingness.

Snow falls.
The arrow flies
to its mark,
unerring, the way
you must become.

Impressions of the rune
Raven Kaldera:

"Yr [is] associated with Aurvandil the famous Norse archer. I've also seen it referred to as the Rune of the Hand, the talisman of artisans, which would place it in the camp of Aurvandil's brother Wayland, the tragic smith. Regardless of which brother lays claim to it, this is a rune of Focus. The total focus of the hunter on the prey, drawing back the bow, closing one eye until his entire being is centered on the task.... This is not that different from the focus of the artist or artisan whose muse is driving them to Create, obsessive hour after obsessive hour, dogged day after dogged day. Each tries to capture something elusive that can only be tracked with the utmost care, patience, and perfect aim. To draw Yr is to bring that focus into your life, whether it is to create or to destroy. You have been scattered long enough, says the Universe; it is now time to discipline your awareness."

––––––––––

Yr is the rune of the craftsman. When it comes up in a reading it usually indicates a need to pay close attention to detail, to leave no proverbial stone unturned, to take the time to do the job right the first time. It cautions one not to rush through anything, but to appreciate the process inherent in crafting something well. This is a rune of mindfulness. It is a rune of hard work, artistry, study, and concentration. Working with this rune and meditating on its nature can help bring those things into one's life. Because it is so strongly associated with keen-eyed focus and excellence in crafting, I also see a connection between it and the Duergar Andvari. Yr is also about allowing yourself to recognize and appreciate proper craftsmanship when you find it without selling yourself or the craftsman short. It cautions that everything should be done in the appropriate time, taking no more or less effort than is required. In this, I can sometimes sense Frau Holle's influence, if only tangentially.

God(s)/dess(es) I associate with Yr:

Aurvandil, Weyland, Andvari, Frau Holle.

Miscellaneous associations:

anvils, hammers, stars, yew, arrows, bows, clocks, watches, day planners (time keepers), ledgers.

Os—Rune of the God-Voice

Traditional meaning: mouth

Phonetic value: ō

Os is a later form of Ansuz.

Anglo-Saxon rune poem:

Os byþ ordfruma ælere spræce,
wisdomes wraþu ond witena frofur
and eorla gehwam eadnys ond tohiht.

The mouth is the source of all language,
a pillar of wisdom and a comfort to wise men,
a blessing and a joy to every knight.

Norwegian rune poem:

Óss er flæstra færða
for; en skalpr er sværða.

Estuary is the way of most journeys;
but a scabbard is of swords.

Icelandic rune poem:

Óss er algingautr
ok ásgarðs jöfurr,
ok valhallar vísi.

God
aged Gautr
and prince of Ásgarðr
and lord of Vallhalla.

Modern rune poem by E. Vongvisith:

A man stands up
before his beloved's father
and speaks. He wins her
and the father's blessing
with his careful words.

Another stands up before
his tribe, to entreat them
not to outlaw his friend.
He does not win, but his
words leave none untouched.

Yet another stands
at the Thing, speaks long.
Silence follows, and then
consultation is made.
Judgment is handed down.

You can only speak
that truth that you know
openly, when the time comes,
and if it is not a truth shared
you are no less worthy
for the speaking.

Impressions of the rune
Raven Kaldera:

"Os is vied for by several deities. It is sometimes associated with Bragi, the skald of the Norse gods, and sometimes with Odin himself when he speaks through a human body. It also has an affinity with Odin's blood brother and arch enemy, Loki the Trickster. What each of these deities has in common is that they represent different ways of speaking divine truths through a human mouth. The skald or bard speaks or sings dramatically, moving the crowd to new emotions. The prophetic voice is often confusing, bringing the stories of the future to the waiting crowd of the moment, but it also important is helping them to touch the divine Wod.

"However, the urge of the Trickster is yet another way in which the God-Voice can work through you. It can be the smooth seductive voice that can persuade Eskimos that ice machines are a good thing, or it can be the uncontrolled fool's voice that asks 'Why?'—even when no one is supposed to notice that things are going wrong, much less comment on them. Loki fools the gods with trickery, but he is also the only one to honestly point out their shortcomings.

"To draw the rune Os is to be told that you must Use Your Words...and they must come from the deepest part of you. You must speak the truth aloud, even if it gets you ostracized. Of course, you're allowed to slant it carefully so that it will be more willingly heard, but you must not compromise the message in the process. The Powers That Be have something that needs to be said, and you are the mouthpiece that they need to say it.

"The glyph of Os is that of a person gesturing, holding forth to an audience. The galdr use for Os is as a talisman of good communication and fine speech. Use it for job interviews, orations, teaching, or anywhere else the gift of words needs to be accessed. Unlike other runes, Os very much seems to like to be eaten; one is reminded of how Iduna carved the runes into Bragi's tongue in order to give him eloquence. Os likes to pass the tongue. I've drawn it on my tongue with ketchup and mustard, drawn them on bread with same and eaten them in a sandwich, and carved them onto cookies that I was baking."

———

Os is a rune of receptivity and inspiration. It is the rune of the oracle, the seer, the truth speaker, the bard. It can be used magically to open oneself up to divine inspiration, particularly poetic inspiration. As Ansuz does, Os cautions one to note well the power of one's words. Words once spoken can never be unspoken; their damage can never be undone. Os teaches that there is no such thing as a careless comment. Words are the sharpest and most dangerous weapons of all. When it comes up reversed in a rune spread, it can indicate blockages in one's relationship with the Gods, blockages in one's ability to effectively communicate, or blockages in one's creativity. In some severely ill-aspected readings, it may indicate malicious slander or gossip.

Os is an excellent rune for singers, actors, and public speakers to meditate on. It is a rune of inspiration, specifically, for inspired speech. It can teach one to use language effectively. It is also an excellent rune to meditate on for spiritual cleansing, as it is this rune's nature to clear away energy blockages and to connect one to one's higher self. For those working in certain branches of Ceremonial Magic, this is the rune to meditate on in order to contact one's HGA.

Os also has the power to see through illusions and, at times, destroy them. It is best accessed and worked through galdr. Although all the runes like to be fed with a few drops of the rune-worker's blood, Os also responds very well to gifts of galdr, chant, or song.

God(s)/Goddess(es) I associate with this rune:

Odin, Loki, Bragi, Saga.

Miscellaneous associations:

harp, musical notes, air symbols, wind, chimes, singing bowls.

 ## Cweorth—Rune of the Funeral Pyre

Phonetic equivalent: \y\, \sw\

There are no traditional rune poems for Cweorth.

Modern rune poem by E. Vongvisith:

As I stand here,
the fire consumes
you whom I once loved.
Your body burns
even as your spirit
ascends or descends
to realms far from Midgard.
All is enveloped in flame
leaving me with ashes.

The field beyond the pyre
is clear, empty and covered
in soft, pure white snow.

Impressions of the rune
Raven Kaldera:

"Cweorth is a glyph of a fire-twirl, the tool used to start sacred fires well after the days of flint and steel. Like Ken/ Kaunaz, it is a rune of Fire, but where Ken is the smith's fire that forges, or the torch of Truth that lights the way, Cweorth is the fire of purification and destruction, the funeral pyre that burns away the dead flesh. The home of all fire in the Norse cosmos is Muspellheim, the fire-world. Its keeper is Surt, the great grim fire giant who engineered the beginning of Midgard, deliberately steering his fiery realm into the ice-world of Niflheim. Surt is the Keeper of the Funeral Pyre, and he is a no-nonsense deity who demands perfection.

"To draw Cweorth is to face the need to purify your life of excesses, strip down, burn away, keep only that which is absolutely necessary to keep on going. Unlike Ear, which is the slow, inevitable entropy, Cweorth is the fiery death that demands your cooperation or you will be burned far worse in the process. (It is interesting to note that the two Death runes correspond to the two sorts of body disposal in Norse times; the upper warrior classes, associated with the Aesir, burned their dead, while the 'straw death' folks who went to Helheim buried theirs.) The galdr usage for Cweorth is to help someone get through such a burning time, and have the strength to excise what needs to go."

This is a rune of dramatic, fiery destruction. It is transformation at its most violent and extreme. There is a tremendous amount of power and energy contained in this rune; in its sheer force, there is a taste of Thurisaz about it. Whereas

Thurisaz speaks of hunger, however, Cweorth is the embodiment of raw fire. This is the rune of Muspelheim, the world of fire. It is both creative and destructive at the same time, for in the act of destruction change occurs and something new is born. Cweorth can be immensely cleansing, but it is a burning, often uncomfortable cleansing. This is untamed fire, the raging forest fire, the unstoppable inferno. This rune can keep us from our own stupidity and greed for excess and will bring the consequences of those things into stark relief. Cweorth often shows us where there has been too much excess, too little focus, a lack of discipline, or too much taking without giving something in return. It is a rune that restores the natural order of things.

Fire by its very nature hallows and consecrates, and Cweorth is no different. This is not a gentle hallowing, however; rather, it is more akin to a scorched-earth approach. It will burn everything in its path indiscriminately. By doing so, Cweorth can bring renewal. This is also the rune of the mysteries of fire. In Norse Cosmology, fire is one of our eldest Ancestors; the world was created by a collision between the world of fire and the world of ice. All fire connects to every fire that has ever been and ever will be. It connects us to the spark or flash of momentum from which creation evolved. It connects us to those Neolithic Ancestors who huddled around a bonfire, dependent on that heat and light to keep predators away, to heat their caves, to cook their food. Fire is an ancient doorway that takes us all the way back to the moment the worlds began. That, too, is contained within Cweorth.

I find this rune to be very positive. It is intense and often uncontrollable, but always immensely passionate. I rarely get the sense in readings that the creative destruction wrought by Cweorth is purposely vicious. It is an example of fire acting according to its nature—nothing more, nothing less. That nature is not malevolent. It simply is.

Gods/Goddesses I associate with this rune:
Surt, Sinmora, Fire Etins, Logi.

Miscellaneous associations:
fire, ash, volcanic glass, fire tools, oil lamps, candles, tiger's eye, obsidian, jet.

The next three runes—Stan, Chalc, and Gar—are all Northumbrian runes.

Stan—The Keystone

Traditional meaning: stone

Phonetic equivalent: \st\, \sht\

There are no traditional rune poems for Stan.

Modern rune poem by E. Vongvisith:

> At the center lies
> solidity, immoveable
> as a great boulder
> buried deep in the earth.
> This firmness provides
> a fulcrum around which
> all things move—
>
> up and down
> like wyrd's vagaries,
> back and forth
> from one end to the other,
> as the center holds firm.
>
> Whatever surrounds this
> hard monolith of reason
> must cling to it, a layer of
> mud mixed with blood,
> pressing towards the stone's heart.

So ask yourself:
what color is the stone,
and is it the true color
or simply that of what cloaks it?

Impressions of the rune
Raven Kaldera:

"Stan (pronounced shtan) means 'stone,' and it is the Rune of the Stone. In this sense, stone refers to the keystone of an arch, or a standing stone, that which stands in the center of the Universe. What is the keystone of your beliefs? Stan asks you to question that, to either reaffirm or abolish it. Wherever it lies in a reading is a key point, the central 'touchstone' of the issue. It may be that the real source of the conflict may be something entirely different from what the parties involved think it is, or are ready to admit.

Stan is an indicator rune, rather like Ansuz which points out a divine message. When you draw Stan for a reading, note the runes just before and after it. These are the keystone of the matter. Its galdr usage is as part of a bind rune to protect something crucial."

———

Stan is a difficult rune to penetrate, in part because, as Kaldera states, it usually shows up in a reading to indicate the importance of the runes that precede and follow it. It is a marker rune, the runic equivalent of the scholar's *nota bene*. It cuts through any facades, any pretense; it is a truth-teller. As a marker stone, it shows the rune-reader the trail that he or she must follow to reach the true problem or issue at hand. As such, it may show up midway through a reading to indicate that the reader is on the right track.

God(s)/Goddess(es) I associate with this rune:
none.

Chalc—The Sacred Chalice

Phonetic equivalent: \k\, \k\

There are no traditional rune poems for Chalc.

Modern rune poem by E. Vongvisith:

> In other worlds, they speak
> of the holiest cup, that which
> captured the sacred blood.
>
> This is your goals,
> the thing which holds
> all that you hold dearest
> but which your hands
> have not yet held.
>
> This is that which contains
> the mead of inspiration,
> or the golden tears of Freya
> or the snake's venom falling
> from a spire of cavern rock.
>
> Your sacred quest—
> decide now if you will
> let the cup remain full
> to the brim, or set it down
> empty, drained of all
> it once quietly contained.

Impressions of the rune
Raven Kaldera:

"Chalc or Calc (pronounced khalk, with a guttural h, though modern people have trouble with that sound and usually just use 'ch') is the Rune of the Chalice. This is the Holy Grail, Arthur's ideal at the end of the quest, and this rune is the ideal that we all strive for. Each person's Holy Grail may be different, but we all have them…or we suffer greatly from lack of that quest. To draw Chalc is to find again that your grasp must exceed your reach, that you may not reach the goal on the horizon, but your life will not be worth much if you don't try.

Chalc has two galdr uses, one high-minded and one rather sleazy. On the one hand, it can be used as a talisman to help you find whatever it is that you are spiritually questing for. On the other hand, it can be applied to an object to temporarily make others desire that thing beyond its real value, which can be used by sleazy salespeople in ways I don't recommend."

———

Chalc often appears in a reading to indicate our highest, greatest desire. It often indicates the potential for spiritual and personal fulfillment. Chalc may represent our deepest passions and inspirations, and our deepest, most secret longings and dreams. There is a certain innocent, untarnished quality to this rune. It is like a child who wishes upon a star, truly believing that the wish will come true. Chalc may point the way to something that one can hold onto when all other dreams have shattered or been lost. It has the power to remind us of who we once were before the grind of living wore us down. A Sigyn's woman once told me that the north star is always within oneself. That is the essence of Chalc.

God(s)/Goddess(es) I associate with this rune:

Freya, Idunna, Sigyn, Tyr.

Miscellaneous associations:

cups, stars, grails, moonstone, rainbow moonstone, pink calcite, tourmaline.

Gar—Odin's Spear

Traditional meaning: Odin's spear (Gungnir)

Phonetic equivalent: \g\

There are no traditional rune poems for Gar.

Modern rune poem by G. Krasskova:

It is my brand, burned in triplicate upon my
flesh,
Carved and blooded, binding me to You.
It is my armor and my shield.
Its three-fold names are many:
Courage, terror, pain,
Ecstasy, devotion, bliss.
It does not matter,
By what name You are called.
It does not matter,
By what words we seek to ward away the storm.
It will come.[2]

Impressions of the rune
Raven Kaldera:

"The final rune, Gar, is not part of the aett. It has no… actual phonetic use. (Some would say 'g,' but that's covered nicely by Gebu/Gyfu.) Some decades ago, when Ralph Blum put together his now-infamous book of Futhark runes, he decided for whatever reason to stick a blank rune at the end of them that was outside of the other aetts. Its meaning was basically that of a "mystery" rune, saying that whatever was happening, you weren't to know. He called it Odin. The Futhark has no such extra blank rune. Why did he feel compelled to create such a thing?

"If he had looked a little further, into the Futhorc, he would have found Gar, which is an actual rune that means exactly that. When I draw Gar, it's usually a sign to stop asking. It's not that the universe isn't set yet, and that things could go many ways—that's more a Peorth sort of thing. It's that for whatever reason, you're not supposed to know. Sometimes knowing something in advance does not have the same impact as actually coming to that wisdom on your own, through experience. That's usually the thrust of Gar, the Spear of Odin.

"I submit that Mr. Blum had a strong hunch that such a rune ought to be there, and that it had something to do with Odin, but he missed the glyph and the name, so he simply left it blank. When folks come to me with Blum-style rune sets and I teach them Futhorc, rather than adding a ninth stone I simply tell them to carve Gar into the blank rune, and it works.

"Gar means spear, referring to Odin's spear, but this is actually a 'kenning' or wordplay on the World Tree, Yggdrasil, the shaft on which Odin hung, speared and bleeding, until he found the Runes. There is no evidence as to what its glyph means, but those who work with it are convinced that it is a picture of the World Tree, Yggdrasil.

To draw Gar is to be told by the Universe that this is not a time to be second-guessing its plans. Instead, one should wait and watch and learn, and let things settle out. The World Tree branches out in many directions, and it is much larger than we are, and we cannot always see what is coming. Instead we must wait, hanging on its branch like Odin, until wisdom chooses to reveal itself to us."

———————

If I am reading someone who is dedicated to Odin, I interpret Gar as Odin's mark, the mark of His spear and the mark of His influence or ownership. Otherwise, it almost always means that one is not supposed to know the answer to the question but, rather, that the knowledge must be won by experience, the process of going through whatever is to come. Gar rarely speaks other than to say, "Stop—this is not yours to know." This rune reeks of Odin, though—His touch, His presence, His influence. There is a whole world of knowledge hidden behind the seal of Gar, but it is tantalizingly just out of reach for the reader and seeker alike. Sometimes it indicates that one must go forward on faith alone. Sometimes it means that this is a test, and the Gods are taking note of how well or poorly we meet whatever challenges lie ahead. Sometimes it means the situation was influenced by the Gods (Odin, usually). Quite often, Gar simply means that an answer isn't going to be given. In this way, it is like the definitive shutting of a door: Nothing the diviner can do will change this.

God(s)/Goddess(es) I associate with this rune: Odin.

Miscellaneous associations: spears, valknots, black, grey, cobalt blue, Yggdrasil, Sleipnir.

5 Wyrd

More than anything else, a rune-worker must have a clear and thorough understanding of Wyrd. The essence of Wyrd underlies every reading, every rune-working, every galdr, every magical working. In fact, Wyrd flows from every single thing a person does, big or small, esoteric or mundane, throughout the course of his or her life. I have often heard Wyrd defined as the Norse concept of karma. Although this is technically true, this is a very simplistic comparison. Wyrd is the essence out of which the fabric of being is woven. It is constantly shifting, constantly inter-connecting, constantly being made and remade by our choices, and constantly impacting us as a direct result of these decisions. Wyrd connects us to all that is, that ever was, and that ever will be. It is the ancestral fabric of all creation. Wyrd simply is. It can be "lived" well or poorly, depending on how one chooses to live one's life. But whether we will or no, Wyrd happens.

> Each one of us is a part of Wyrd and so it follows that our choices, reflecting us as they do, will impact Wyrd. In this sense, there is no such thing as a trivial choice.

Today I bought a box of regular tissues instead of my usual, recycled ones because I had forgotten to buy them at the health food store. Not only did this have an environmental impact, it wove a more lethargic, more indifferent Fuensanta into the tapestry of Wyrd. Yesterday I chose to listen with what kindness I could muster, to a friend whose concerns seemed to me to be absurd. That choice changed me also, and so changed Wyrd. Some of these repercussions are based on ethics, some are not. If during my spare time, I choose to listen to my favorite music, this will put me in a different frame of mind than if I choose to go for a walk. There is no better or worse, just different. A slightly different Fuensanta, a slightly different thread in that web into which we weave ourselves, hour after hour, day after day.[1]

The cosmological image of Wyrd is that of a vast inter-locking web woven and maintained by three women—the Nornir, or Fates. The first of these mighty women is Urda, who governs the past, ordering the layers of Wyrd in the Well of Memory. The second Norn is Verdande, she who is becoming. Verdande is the Norn of the present, that which is coming into being and bridging the gap between Urda and the youngest Norn, Skuld. Skuld governs causality and consequence. She cuts the threads of one's life, determining not only when it will end but also when consequences for one's decisions, good or ill, will come due.[2] The three Nornir sit by Yggdrasil, near the Well of Memory, and work the web of Wyrd. Their actions and care nourish Yggdrasil, the World-Tree, which in turn supports creation. It is important to note that the Nornir do not create the patterns of Wyrd; they order what is being patterned and created by us. We each create our own patterns, be they convoluted or clear, based on the type of lives we choose to live. Personal responsibility and accountability are hallmarks of Wyrd.

Of course, the Nornir don't just weave, measure, order, and cut threads of personal Fate. They also govern cosmological law. They determine what is lawful and unlawful, an esoteric concept that goes well beyond good and evil. That which is lawful is that action which may be undertaken without incurring destructive, harmful consequences. That which is unlawful is that which if undertaken, will tip one's Wyrd into the negative, incurring difficult and complicated debt. An action may be positive and still not be lawful. Conversely an action may be quite destructive but, in the eyes of the Nornir, based on the balance of Wyrd, be completely and thoroughly lawful. Sometimes it can seem frighteningly gray to the rune-worker. Lawfulness and unlawfulness is all about maintaining a proper balance, not only of one's personal Wyrd, but also of the greater, larger tapestry of woven threads—the universal Wyrd. Working magic with these concepts in mind is rather like playing a vast game of chess in which you are expected to calculate the effects of your moves well in advance of your actions.

Wyrd is remarkably interactive. It both influences us and flows from us. We can actually inherit Wyrd from our forebears and based on how we cope with this, we have the potential to leave an inheritance of Wyrd-debt that is better or worse for our descendants. We can affect our ancestral Wyrd by working hard, with diligence and honor, and by living mindfully and with integrity and bearing up under whatever complicated circumstances come our way. Wyrd is both causality and consequence, ever-shifting and ever-changing. It is the sum total of cosmological, ancestral, and universal memory. As I wrote in Exploring the Northern Tradition, it is a web of choices—one's own choices, the choices of others, the choices of one's community, and even the choices of one's Ancestors affecting one's current evolution and awareness.[3]

Wyrd orders everything. The process of its weaving and ordering is the ongoing flow of living and dying. How you choose to die by action or omission also impacts Wyrd. A gifted rune-worker can interact with Wyrd on a unique level. When one divines for a person, one is engaging in what the Norse called spae—the process of reading the threads by sight, by touch, and by awareness to discover information, read history, and access memory, potentiality, and possibility. It is important to realize that everyone interprets energy differently. Some people are gifted seers, while others achieve the same results by sensing or feeling or even through sound. When a diviner looks into the future during a reading, he or she is not reading a Fate that is absolutely set and unchangeable; rather, the diviner is reaching into a vast flowing network of possibilities and potentialities and, based on past choices, patterns, and threads, determining the most likely outcome. That outcome can change. For this reason, more than any other, divination is a fluid art. One skilled diviner I know once called it "the art of interpreting the endlessly shifting flow of possibilities."

Often the diviner will see a clear course of action that could be taken to affect the situation at hand. Sometimes he or she will also see what, if any, impact ancestral Wyrd is having on the current situation. Doing this well requires a certain comfort level with abstractions, symbolic language, and metaphorical concepts. It can seem distressingly nebulous at times. However, Wyrd is a concrete reality for rune-workers, not just during the process of divination but also (perhaps especially) during the working of magic.

The practice of magic will be discussed in a later chapter; suffice it to say that the threads of Wyrd form a network of conduits and pathways into which runes can be cast to affect a specific target, be it a person or a situation. Gaining access in order to do this is another matter altogether and depends largely on the state of one's own Wyrd, one's relationship with the other worlds, and, especially, one's relationship with the runes themselves. In nearly 20 years, I've known only a handful of rune-magicians who could do so and only with varying levels of skill. The threads of Wyrd are the veins and arteries of existence, the metaphysical, spiritual, and esoteric DNA of the individual, which can be poisoned for good or for ill. There is, however, always a price for even attempting to do so.[4]

For those people who are neither magicians nor diviners, Wyrd can be worked best by striving to live honorably and well, by keeping ones word, by honoring the Gods and Ancestors, and by upholding one's commitments to the best of one's ability. For those magicians and diviners who work predominantly with the runes, however, understanding and developing a keen sensitivity to the flows and balance of Wyrd is essential.

6 Galdr

aldr, from the Old Norse verb *gala*, which means "to crow, to cry, to scream," and the noun *gal*, which means "screaming" or "howling," is a form of magical song or chant common to Northern Tradition magic. It is an incredibly potent form of magical practice, one in which the voice itself becomes the conduit for the power the vitki is raising. Galdr most often goes hand-in-hand with runes; the twinning of these two forces can be tremendously potent.

When a person galdrs, it isn't a matter of just stringing notes together; there is form, pattern, rhythm, and intent. The rune is expressing itself, telling a story and taking both the singer and the listener(s) someplace. It is revealing its essence. When someone galdrs, one doesn't just hear galdr; one experiences it through all the senses: sight, taste, touch, and so on. The entire sensorium should be involved, and all should flow through both the singer and listener. Sound is merely the most immediate medium that the rune uses to open you up to the totality of what it is, what it wants you to experience, and what it wishes to reveal. The voice becomes the key to opening up the world of the runes, the doorway to the web of Wyrd, and the creative and destructive power of *Ginungagap*, the primal void from which all life sprang.

The runes are composed of sacred power. On a purely mundane level, we know the power of sound, and the power of the voice in particular. Just think of Ella Fitzgerald shattering glass with a single note, or consider the fact that many governments today are using sonic technologies as weapons. When that degree of power is combined with the sacred power and intelligence of the runes, the tonal energies and vibrations of galdr open points of connection to the multiverse on the web. It impacts the web and the listener on a subatomic level. It moves into and through its intended target in a way that is not easily blocked or deflected.

An acquaintance of mine believes that we all have an inborn template of sorts, a part of our psyche that responds viscerally to certain musical phrases and notes. Although he doesn't know where it comes from, he believes this is one of the reasons for the primal power of music, noting its deep impact on cultures the world over. No culture, after all, is without its musical tradition. This inborn affinity for music might be an expression of natural algorithms, the musical equivalent of mathematical formulae that are found everywhere in nature (for example, the Fibonacci sequence). Certain occultists at the turn of the last century believed this as well. This makes galdr an incredibly powerful bridge between the world of temporal manifestation and the world of the Wyrd-web. It also makes it an incredibly potent tool when it is used for either healing or harm on the psycho-emotional level.

In fact, it is almost as though by uniting the runes with the rhythm, power, and vibrations of the voice that a separate state of being is created. Therefore the galdr singer must learn to move along and navigate within this new energy. The voice inhabits the personality of whomever is galdring it. All worlds have beings that galdr. Jotun galdr sounds nothing like human galdr, and Elven galdr sounds nothing like Jotun galdr. When we galdr, we infuse the rune with the energies of our world and form a link from our world to the web. The runes lack that connective ability on their own. The energy of our galdr, combined with the energy of the runes, creates a bridge, which then becomes an experience of the rune defined through Midgard's being and essence. The runes can travel through all realms but cannot create the bridges and doorways themselves. For that, they need the galdr and the willing vitki.

How to Galdr

The best way to learn galdr is to practice it with the runes. The runes will teach and test the singer, and there is no better way to learn. Select a rune (and be prepared for it to ask for blood for its aid) and sit or stand comfortably. Visualize the rune in your mind's eye. Feel it filling you, coming to life within you, surging through your blood, taking over your heartbeat, whispering its rhythm in your ear. Let it surge upward until it bubbles up in your throat, and allow its power to exit via your voice. See where it wants to go. Take note of any sounds, images, and even smells that come to you as you are chanting. What should one actually chant? Well, starting with the name of the rune is good. From there, work the images or sounds that come to mind while focusing on the rune into the actual galdr. I never plan galdr out beforehand. It is a living, changing, fluid thing. Eventually, you'll get to the point where even the actual name of the rune is too constraining. At that point, the galdr becomes comprised of pure, raw, primal sound.

If you have never sung before (and galdr is halfway between chanting and singing, with a healthy dose of screeching!) this exercise may seem difficult, awkward, and even embarrassing. If this is the case, work on building up a comfort level in making your voice heard. Practice basic singing exercises like singing the vowels, maintaining a single note for each vowel.

Sing scales and sing your prayers. I don't necessarily advocate taking singing lessons because, again, too much focus on making the galdr aesthetically pleasing will destroy it. It is what it is: harsh, beautiful, frightening, cruel, intense, raw, and pure. It's important to allow it to be what it wants to be and to not project our own sense of aesthetics onto it. All in all, though, galdr is best learned by doing.

There are several other important factors to keep in mind with this art. Firstly, there is a reason its etymology comes from a verb meaning "to crow." Galdr can be incredibly dissonant. One need not have a nice, pleasing, or pretty voice to be an accomplished galdr master. Emphasis on making the melody beautiful can detract from the power of the magic itself. The sound of galdr is the sound of the runes flowing over and into the web of Wyrd itself. It reflects the vibrations of those threads. Therefore, what we are hearing is, at best, distorted.

Secondly, the galdr will guide the singer. Once a person begins to galdr with the intent of infusing a rune and a specific purpose into the web, a pattern will emerge on the threads of Wyrd which will then become visible to the singer. The galdr will want to hit specific openings and fill specific gaps, creating its own warp and weft against the weave of the web itself. This may put extreme strain on the vocal abilities of the singer, but in time, the voice will strengthen and gain in flexibility (though not necessarily in any euphonic sense!).

Thirdly, galdr may be practiced alone or in a group of galdr singers. In a group, one person should lead, controlling the beginning, the distribution of energy into the threads, and the ending of the common chant. Some people may find that they have a unique ability to harmonize and balance the energies in a group galdr-working. They may or may not have the same ability when galdring by themselves. In this case, it's not so much about vocal harmonizing the way a singer would, but about harmonizing the energy.

Magician S. Reicher notes:

"One should of course, ground and center thoroughly before beginning any galdr practice. Centering is not difficult. The first exercise is one that I originally learned in a martial arts class. It has many uses. It is very simple. All you do is focus on your breathing. Inhale four counts, hold four counts, exhale four counts, hold four counts. That's all. Do it over and over repeating the pattern without breaks. Try to time it to your heart beat but if that is too distracting don't worry about it and just breathe. In time, as you breathe, you want to feel all the breath, all the energy in your body gathering behind your naval. Eventually, as you breathe, you want to feel the energy gathering in a glowing golden ball at this point. Basically, centering is 'contemplating your naval'! Be sure to breathe through your diaphragm taking deep, even breaths. Centering can be very calming when under stress. If you find yourself in an emotionally stressful situation, it may help to fall into this breathing pattern."[1]

Reicher continues with an exercise in grounding:

"Now, once the energy in your body has been collected, it has to go somewhere. Grounding adds stability, it gives one a connection to the earth. Basically grounding is just sending all the energy that has been collected in the body, down into the earth. Don't worry if you can't see or feel anything...start with the mental focus and eventually your awareness of the internal flow of energy will increase.

"Grounding isn't hard either. It's occasionally boring, but not difficult. The easiest exercise to begin with is also, like centering, a breathing exercise. Inhale and feel the energy gathered in your center. Now, as you exhale, feel that energy exiting the body through the perineum. On the second exhale, feel it entering the earth and branching out into a thick, sturdy network of roots. Continue this imagery for as long as you need to [with] each ensuing exhalation taking you further and further into the earth until you feel fully grounded. Grounding provides stability and can help prevent one from becoming overwhelmed by the energies one is working with.

"The idea with grounding is to be a tree. Once you've gathered the energy at your naval, send it down into the earth. Send all the energy down, timing it to each exhalation, into the earth. See it streaming from your root chakra in a solid golden cord of energy. This cord goes down through the floor, through the foundations of the house and into the earth, it reaches very deeply and with each exhalation see it branching off like roots of a tree, tying you tightly to the earth. A variation on this is to ground yourself by sending that cord of energy into the Well of Urda rather than the earth. It gives a far more fluid and flexible ground. In time you will learn to pull energy up through this ground as well."[2]

These are invaluable exercises, and any exploration of magic should begin with a commitment to regular daily practice. These exercises are so important that when I began my occult training in the early 1990s, I spent a solid year doing almost nothing but grounding, centering, and cleansing. These simple exercises are fundamental.

The uses of galdr work are manifold. I have used galdr as an offering to feed specific Deities. I have used it to work both woe and weal. I've used it to stop bleeding, to heal wounds, to hallow a particular place or space, to induce shape-shifting in a berserk, to induce trance- and journey-work, and to connect to Odin on the Tree at the moment of His greatest anguish. Galdr is also one of the single most effective ways of accessing and developing a relationship with the runes. And because it provides fairly direct access to the web, it can create tremendous paradigm shifts with very little effort. It is one of the most effective tools for luck workings; one need not even be near one's intended target for galdr to strike home quickly and efficiently.

At its best, galdr is a full-body experience. The body itself, not just the voice, becomes a conduit for the rune and its power. The power expressed does not just flow outward into the web; it first flows through the body of the singer, through each and every molecule. It leaves its mark and will pattern the singer to both the runes and a greater awareness of the flow and patterning of Wyrd. I don't believe this patterning can be undone. Due to its raw power, should a galdr singer lose control of the galdr or break off before the galdr is complete, the backlash can be rather severe. It is one of the more dangerous of the runic arts and not something a beginner should attempt. Because the body itself becomes a tool, the singer should take care to keep him- or herself in as healthy a condition as possible. After an intense session of galdr (or any magical or trance-working for that matter), the practitioner may find him- or herself experiencing a number of physical tics: twitching, shaking, spasming, and/or jerking. This is normal. In Hindu yogic practices, these are called *kriyas*. They're energy spasms, the body's way of ridding itself of excess energy that would otherwise overwhelm one's physical and psychic channels. The best thing to do is to allow it to happen while focusing on grounding.

Galdr work goes hand-in-hand with blood magic and rune-work. This powerful combination forms the foundation for Northern Tradition runic magic. Its efficacy is attested to not only by Odin's ordeal on the Tree but in the sagas, as well. In the end, it will bring one to Odin as few other things will. It is a potent magical practice.

7 Divination

A mongst the overwhelming majority of rune-workers today, the primary use for the runes is for divination. Divination is the casting of runes, either by throwing them down or by selecting them individually and at random, in order to read the threads of Wyrd, to unravel fate, and to bring clarity to a particular issue or issues for the person being read. This type of work has its precedent in ancient times in a variety of cultures, wherein divination was viewed as a sacred skill, one that required both aptitude and training. As early as 98 CE, Roman historian Tacitus described the casting of lots and other forms of prophetic work amongst the Germanic tribes.[1] He also notes that women gifted with "prophetic sense" were revered almost as though they were divine themselves.[2]

Divination is an art, and it takes understanding, skill, and perseverance to practice this art well. It requires not only a strong reciprocal ongoing relationship with the runes, but also a strong sensitivity to Wyrd (both of which can be developed). Ideally, the diviner also has an inborn talent for precognition, emotion-sensing, and/or energy-sensing. Such talents are often inherited and are no more remarkable than inheriting eye color or hair color. If such a talent is latent, it can often be developed through diligent practice and working with the runes.

When one reads tarot, the cards are not living spirits. They are visual metaphors that help the reader key him- or herself into his or her gift of precognition. Runes are a little different. Part of being a good rune-reader is not just learning the language of the runes, but learning to interpret it in a way that makes sense to the person being read (often called a querent). This is where one's alliance with the runes is invaluable. Wyrd is dynamic, alive, and always shifting, sometimes very rapidly. A gifted seer can read its patterns and convey the information found there, but the runes can take that one step further: They can speak directly to the seer, bringing information to light that may not be readily apparent from an overview of the Wyrd-patterns.

In this way, conducting a reading is very similar to holding a conversation with the rune spirits. There's a massive amount of give and take involved. It's not just a matter of passively interpreting what is seen, but of querying the runes, allowing them to investigate, and then relaying what they find to the querent. It's a much more complex process than one might think. Reading with the runes, when one has a relationship with them, is a process of continually negotiating with them and with one's ability to read Wyrd. Interpreting all of this information for the client may not be particularly straightforward either. Often, information does not come to the reader through words. There is sight, feeling, sound, taste, smell, images, sensation. Wyrd, like energy, can be transmitted to the reader in a myriad of different ways depending on the individual reader's mental filters and the way they relate to his or her sensorium (in other words, which of his or her senses is dominant). This is why I emphasize that doing this work well is a matter of learning to interpret the information one is receiving in a way that makes sense to the client. It's all a process of negotiation.

There's one more thing that novice readers should be aware of: Once a reading is done, it always exists. It is present in the Wyrd. It holds space and shape and form. A reading can never be undone. An experienced diviner or Wyrd-worker can go back through the threads and flow of Wyrd and touch that reading again, accessing it at a later time to be "read" as one would read a book. Even in this, we leave undeniable evidence of where we've been. For this reason more than any other, I urge diviners not to read on unimportant topics. The runes are not spiritual vending machines designed to dispense answers to every little nagging question of life. They may only be consulted for those questions of true import. This is a matter of respect for one's art and one's allies. Think hard about whether or not the matter at hand is important enough to muck about in Wyrd.

Over the years, I have learned better than to simply grab my runes and sit down to read without any preamble or preparation at all. Under duress I might do this, but I've learned that it's usually best to prepare myself for the process of reading. I look at it much as I would look at bathing and dressing properly to meet an important acquaintance. One doesn't just run out the door without proper grooming! Preparing appropriately for a reading, whether for oneself or for a client, helps the diviner get into the most effective mindset both to hear the runes, read the Wyrd, and access the necessary information. Sometimes I won't have much notice before a reading. I may be meeting with a client and we will realize mid-meeting that divination is necessary. In that case, I take a few moments to center myself and perhaps offer a prayer—for example, "May Wyrd show rightly what is writ for all to see. May I have the understanding to interpret it, and the wisdom to know when to speak and when to stay silent. May the Gods guide my tongue and may I be blessed with clarity of vision." Then I hold my runes, sending energy and intent into them, draw them out, and read. I can certainly just sit down and read if I have to; I have done so quite often in the past. However, if I know in advance that I will be doing divination for someone, I prefer to prepare far more thoroughly.

Granted, these preparations are more for putting me into a receptive frame of mind than they are for the runes. Yet that is a necessary part of being a good diviner: knowing how and when to become receptive to Wyrd, to the runes, and to one's gifts. So if I know that I'm going to be doing a reading for someone, I eat very lightly beforehand. Food is very grounding, and although I need to be able to ground consciously, I do not want heaviness or a feeling of fullness to distract me from my work. I may spend part of the day resting or in meditation, or I may take a cleansing bath with infusions of special herbs or anoint myself with smoke from a stick of dried mugwort. (Mugwort is mentioned in Anglo-Saxon healing texts in this context, and amongst spirit-workers, the plant is associated with opening one's spirit-sight and dispelling negative energy.) Before a reading you need to be clean in every possible sense of the word. Certainly, I will pray to Odin as I am His, and if I know my client belongs to a specific Deity, I may seek out that Deity, as well. I keep myself open to the presence and inspiration of my Gods. I may even talk to the runes beforehand about the upcoming reading.

I will also take precautions for the space in which I am reading precisely because a good reading involves opening oneself up. I can read anywhere, but again, my preference is to have clients come to me and to read them in my workroom. I am fortunate in that I can set aside a specific room to see clients, perform readings, work magic, and so on. Nine times out of 10, preparing the room is not all that necessary. That 10th time, however, will make you wish you had been doing it all along. I find it useful to ward, not only because clients may be bringing bad energy into your space, but also because they may not be alone. Sometimes clients will come to you with very active spirits around them. Sometimes their presence is good and natural (for example, the person's Ancestors may be particularly active and protective of them). Sometimes, however, it is infestation in the most negative sense of the word, and the spirits involved may not have the client's best interests at heart. For this reason alone, I ward my space. Part of reading is being receptive to external influences (the runes, the Gods), and it's important and wise to make sure that one is not receptive to negative spirit influence.

Spirits can be as sneaky as hell, and will often behave in unethical and surprisingly self-destructive ways. For those of you who, like me, offer divination as part of your services, this is an important thing to know. When a person divines, the reader enters into a state of psychic receptivity. Sometimes there are very good and lawful reasons for a spirit to come and give information to a diviner. There are spirit-workers out there who are owned by or in service to non-Deity spirits and although these spirits are usually ancestral, that is not always the case. Extra care must be taken by the diviner whenever a spirit comes to a reading. Why? Because the spirit can linger well after the reading, and if the reader remains receptive (as many of us do for the first hour or so following a reading), he or she can be dangerously vulnerable to outside influence. It's very easy for a determined spirit to influence a diviner into doing something stupid, unwise, or dangerous if the diviner doesn't realize this is possible. Never underestimate a hungry spirit. They can make themselves appear ever so altruistic and friendly, but *always* question their motives. The best house wards in the world won't help if you've invited a spirit in.

The real work begins after the reading. Be especially aware of any ideas that come to your mind after a reading in which a non-Deity spirit has been present, particularly when those ideas are ones that will either involve or benefit that spirit.

Do not ever neglect to do divination should you suddenly find yourself absolutely certain that this spirit must be called again or some ritual done for its benefit. Most of all, assume nothing. Do not assume that the people coming into your space have protections or wards, even if they are experienced magicians or mediums. I have seen particularly powerful spirits subtly and insidiously influence very skilled occultists to leave all their protective gear at home before a ritual. If one is not expecting it, such influence can be devastating. I don't say this to frighten potential diviners. I say it because forewarned is forearmed.

There are a few very simple things that one can do to ward one's space against negative spirits. Most of these practices come from southern-style Hoodoo, in which the use of herbs and powders for such things is routine. Why do I use Hoodoo when I'm a Northern Traditionalist? It's effective, period. I'm very pragmatic and very lazy. If I can accomplish an effective house-warding without expending any of my own personal energy, I'll do it. So, here are a few simple things that readers can do to keep their space clean:

- Put a bowl of water in each corner of the room. Empty them immediately after your client leaves.

- Set out a container of red vinegar. This is an old trick to prevent negative spirit manifestation. I've no idea why it works but I've found it to be effective.

- Smudge the room with mugwort or another cleansing herb (cedar, sage, and tobacco blended together work well) before the client arrives and after he or she leaves.

- After the client leaves, put a square of camphor in each corner of the room, then go and take a cleansing bath or smudge yourself with a cleansing herb.

>> Call to your Gods, your Ancestors, and any protective spirits you have alliance with before the reading commences and ask them/Them to protect and ward the space.

>> Light a candle and talk to the fire spirits, asking them to keep the space cleansed and purified. Fire by its very nature purifies.

>> Sprinkle Florida water around the room at the end of a reading.

>> Consecrate the space or do a hammer hallowing (if that's part of your practice) or some similar protective rite before the client arrives.

I do all of this and more as a matter of course. Once your client leaves, cleanse yourself again, perhaps spending a bit of time centering and grounding, praying, and whatever you feel you need to do. Then eat something and do something completely mundane to effect the transition back to a mundane state of mind.

Compared to the preparation required, the actual process of reading is fairly simple. First, ask the querent what his or her primary question is. Most people come to diviners with an issue already in mind. Hold the bag with your runes and concentrate on the question, infusing the runes with your intent. I usually get a sense of when the runes are ready to answer. It's almost as if they want to be wanted, to be courted. The energy and intent that you feed them at this time is part of your payment to them for their answers. When you sense intuitively that they're ready to be thrown or drawn, either reach into your bag (some people prefer to put them in a bowl) and grab a handful and throw them down, or select individual runes and lay them out in a pattern.[3]

If you are throwing down a handful of runes, they may be read slightly differently than if you are using a pattern, though the end result is the same. In both cases, it's not necessarily about individual runes (though a single rune can speak loudly and clearly in a reading, too) but the pattern of the whole—how the runes interrelate and how and what they are communicating—that conveys the necessary information. Don't rush into interpretation. Don't feel that you have to begin speaking immediately. Look at the runes, individually and together. Feel out the Wyrd. Talk to them if you have to, even out loud. You'll feel the reading open to you. Sometimes this happens slowly and sometimes all at once in a great rush. Regardless, wait for that point and don't allow the presence of the querent to rush you into premature interpretation.

Reading for someone else, especially if you are very new to the process, can be intimidating. Approach your craft with humility but also with the knowledge that you've worked long and hard to gain the right to read, and you've acquire the necessary skill to do so well. Your only obligation is to state what you are receiving as clearly as possible and to be equally clear when you are uncertain of something (particularly if you feel your own experience may be clouding your judgment). Be as up-front and clear as possible. If you don't know how to interpret an image or a sensation, simply tell the client what you're getting. Sometimes he or she will have the key to the interpretation. What may be senseless to you may make perfect sense to him or her. You are not responsible for whether or not the querent likes what you say. Your job is not to make them feel good by saying what they want to hear; your job is to speak what you see, hear, and/or sense. Moreover, you are not responsible for whether or not they act on your advice. You are an interpreter. What they do with the knowledge and how they react to it is on them, not you. Just do your job as cleanly as possible. Keep your ego out of it.

Reading for oneself can be problematic for this very reason. It can be difficult to maintain the necessary objectivity to correctly hear and interpret the runes. Furthermore, if one is deeply afraid of a particular outcome and cannot step back from that fear, or if one deeply desires a particular outcome and cannot step back from that desire, the pull of that unfettered emotion can skew the reading dramatically. The runes can latch onto it and confuse the reader. Excellence in reading comes from a combination of several factors: acquired skill, innate gift, receptivity, and, perhaps most of all, *personal detachment*. If this latter factor is missing, the runes may take that as carte blanche to tease, trick, or play with the reader. On a purely psychological level, if we lack detachment, our interpretation will be subjective and hence less reliable. In issues of deep emotional import, it's best to seek out a colleague and have him or her do the divination.

There is no right or wrong way to lay the runes out. Some people have specific spreads that they like to use; others simply throw the runes down and read whatever comes out face up. I tend to do whatever feels right at the time. Sometimes I throw a handful of runes down. Sometimes I draw individual runes and lay them out in specific patterns. If I come up with a pattern I like, I write it down so I can use it later.

Past-Present-Future Spread

A very common spread is the past-present-future spread:

The first rune represents the past influences on a situation; the second rune represents what's going on in the present, where the querent is now; and the third rune represents the future outcome. This is a very simple and to-the-point spread. It's a good pattern to use if you are reading for yourself. It's also useful when giving an overview of the querent's situation prior to delving further into the Wyrd with other readings.

Double Chevron Spread

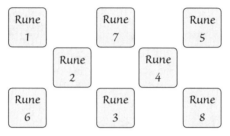

Runes 2, 3, 4, and 7 represent internal influences on the situation that are stemming from the querent. Runes 1, 5, 6, and 8 represent external influences that exist independent of the querent. When working this spread be sure to also read the overall pattern, because the way the runes respond to and interact with each other can be very enlightening. It is also important to read the two chevrons separately—runes 1 through 5 and then runes 6 through 8. Doing this reveals different layers of the relevant Wyrd.

Hammer Spread

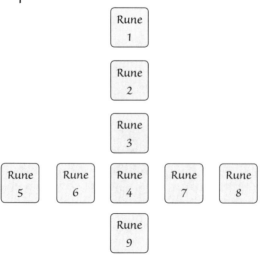

This is a particularly good spread for reading spirit-workers, God-touched folks, mystics, Shamans, and the like because it focuses on revealing the spiritual pattern that may be underlying a given situation. Runes 1 through 4 speak to that overall spiritual lesson, pattern, or challenge. Runes 5, 6, 7, and 8 reveal the physical/temporal manifestations of that pattern. Rune 9 should be laid down last, along with the query: "Is there anything else we should know?"

The Nine Worlds Spread

This is one of my favorite spreads. I'm sure I'm not the first rune-reader to use this spread, but when the inspiration struck last year to do it this way, I was delighted with the results. I couldn't figure out why I hadn't thought of it sooner!

The reader may work from the bottom up (Helheim to Asgard) or from the top down (Asgard to Helheim). The runes should be laid out around a vertical axis, with one rune for each of the nine worlds:

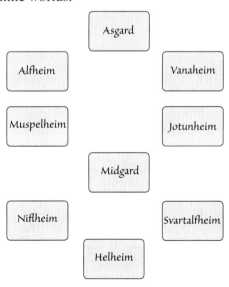

>> Asgard represents the Aesir, one's mental outlook, one's connection to the Gods, and the driving motivation behind one's actions (including pride, courage, cowardice, and so on).

>> Alfheim represents creativity, whether it is blocked or not. It can also speak to the glamours and masks one wears, for good or ill. Deception, lies, beauty, and imagination are all bound up in the lessons of Alfheim.

>> Vanaheim is all about wealth, abundance, sexuality, body issues, food issues, and how we nourish and are nourished by the world around us. It is also passion, envy, jealousy, and hospitality.

>> Muspelheim is fire—raw passion, creative force, inspiration, action, choice, one's energy, vitality, and health.

>> Midgard is about how we are in the world. Issues of embodiment, including the tension between community/conformity and individuality, are likely to come out here.

>> Jotunheim is primal force, anger issues, shadow work, those parts of ourselves we may not want to look at, and a need for discipline vs. a need for spontaneity. Balancing one's individuality with the needs of community may also be an issue here.

>> Niflheim may indicate survival issues, entropy, ennui, lack of focus, need for action, ruthlessness, selfishness, compassion, and the proper use of resources on all levels.

>> Not unexpectedly, Helheim deals with ancestral issues, apathy vs. action, peace, balance, and harmony (both a need for these things and how to get them). Helheim can show the root of the matter at hand.

It's important not to get too caught up in how to lay the runes down. Usually I don't follow any particular pattern; I just lay them out however I'm moved to do so at the time. Only occasionally does the pattern seem to be of any import. Often the runes themselves will indicate where they want to go (almost like a physical manifestation of what occurs in galdr, in which the runes point to the notes the galdr-worker's voice should hit). Additionally, there may be times that the runes simply refuse to read for a querent. They may or may not share the reasons for their refusal, but it's best not to force the issue. Either refer the client to someone else or use a different system of divination. (I keep a lithomancy set and tarot cards in my diviner's kit for just such a purpose.)

One little discussed use for reading runes is for help in dialoguing with one's Gods. Shamans, spirit-workers, and other God-touched folk work long and hard to insure that they will hear their Gods as accurately and clearly as possible. They use a plethora of practices and tools to maintain a clear and open channel of communication. Not everyone is a Shaman, spirit-worker, or God-touched person, however, and even among those who are, there are always those times when one's signal is not as clear as one might wish. Sometimes it can be very difficult to know what the Gods want from us. During those times, the runes can be used to facilitate communication and ferret out messages. I have known more than one person who was neither a Shaman nor a priest nor a spirit-worker, but who used the runes effectively in this way. It's very different from working with the runes directly, however. Here, the runes are an intermediary between the reader (who in this case is also the querent) and forces much bigger than even than the runes themselves: the Holy Powers. Heathen author and mystic Fuensanta Arismendi says it better than I ever could:

> There are Runes and then there are runes. Spirit workers have access to the former. The vast majority of us have access to the latter: runes as an emergency

phone line to and from the Gods. Some general rules might be useful to beginners. First and foremost, remember your manners. This may seem strange advice, but if we are to use runes as a phone, we should remember we're calling upon our betters. So do not pester the Gods with trivial questions. Keep your "conversation" short and to the point, and learn to take "no" for an answer.

I find the best way to use the runes is to hold the open bag of runes with one hand, ask of my Gods, "What happens if I do X? Please my lord/my lady give me an answer I can understand." Then I put my hand in the bag and seek until a rune feels right and pull it out. Next I ask, "What happens if I don't do X?" and repeat the process. It is worth noting that "what happens" really means "what do you think of my doing/not doing X?" as well as "what will be the outcome?" The request that the answer be one we can understand is important. As a wise Odin's man once noted, "Sometimes we have to remind the Gods that we're human." If the answer is unclear, try one more time. One. More. Time. If it is still unclear, give thanks and drop the subject.

If you're having a crisis of faith, do not attempt to solve it by pulling runes. This is the equivalent of saying, "Excuse me, Sir, Ma'am, in whom I don't believe right now, could your possibly nonexistent presence come to the phone?" Instead, make use of the amazing quote from, of all places, the Bible: "Lord, I believe, help thou my unbelief." And wait. Faith is like the tide, it ebbs and flows. Ask if you want, but ask not overmuch. Often we know full well the answer to our query. Many questions are solved by simply doing one's duty. Still, we ask in the hope the answer will exonerate us. Usually it won't. So only ask when you have a burning question.

Shamans may do divination on the same subject, or spirit workers, several times because the threads of Wyrd are in constant change. Not so the Gods reply! If you don't like the answer, it is still the answer. Don't whine. Don't argue. Do not attempt elaborate spreads as fervor tends to get lost in the process and the only thing holding the phone line open is your fervor. Unlike shamans, I find the blank "rune" indispensable, not as some writers would have it, as a find of unfathomable mystery. Perthro has that meaning. To me, the blank "rune" is my way of telling the Gods that I am aware They need not answer the phone. The blank "rune" means nothing at all, no reply to our query. Without it, a response becomes unavoidable and I consider this to be of the utmost impertinence towards the Gods: as though They were at our beck and call bound to answer our every question.

It is important to realize that both systems, the Runes and the runes, coincide. A shaman friend once called me with a request that I pull runes on an important matter: whether to stay in a hated job or leave that job to become a full time student, which would require a tremendous leap of faith. Since my friend was at work, she had no access to her Runes. I prayed to my Gods, and asked: "What happens if she leaves her job?" and pulled out berkana. I did not even ask the second question, the first had been so fully answered. That evening, my friend wanted to double check with the Runes and berkana flew out of the bag.

I actually keep two sets of runes: one in my diviner's kit, which I use when reading clients, and one on my altar, which I use in those rare times when I question my signal clarity and have no access to a colleague to call on.

Having the ability to access Wyrd, whether to read it or actively alter it, raises many ethical questions that every diviner has to face sooner or later. This is imperative when that diviner becomes a community resource and begins taking clients. The people coming to you for readings will often be in a state of stress and desperate need. They're looking for answers. Sometimes they desperately need answers and sometimes they need to be told some hard truths. Sometimes there's a frighteningly fine line between divination and therapy or spiritual direction. This is sacred work and it needs to be treated as such, especially by the diviner in question. To paraphrase the Hippocratic oath, at the very least let us strive to do no harm.

To some degree, developing a working code of ethics and finding those lines that one simply will not cross is an ongoing process. In this art, as in many others, we learn by doing. We all come to this work from very different backgrounds, and each person's code of behavior and ethics will evolve as his or her understanding and experience evolves. Problems and issues will inevitably arise, but, ideally, the diviner will learn from his or her mistakes. He or she can also learn valuable lessons from colleagues, especially those who have been doing this work for a long time. Networking with other respected and skilled diviners can be an invaluable learning tool, one that is all too often overlooked or undervalued. At the very least, approach what you do with respect. Understand that by engaging in a reading for a client, you are in a position to impact that client emotionally and, by extension, psychologically. It helps to keep a strong and ongoing relationship with the Gods through regular devotional practice and prayer. It helps to keep a strong relationship with the runes through regular offerings. But more than anything else, it helps to always be mindful and respectful.

My colleague Raven Kaldera, an experienced diviner in his own right (I believe he currently knows more than 27 different forms of divination), offers the following guidelines for community diviners:

1. A community diviner should be well-trained. Ideally she should know more than one system of divination, because no one system works for every client. She should be experienced at each system, enough to be able to do it in times of stress and trouble.

2. A community diviner should be objective, including being objective about his lack of objectivity. He should be able to tell when his own feelings or opinions are getting in the way of giving a particular client the cleanest reading possible, and be able to humbly refer them to someone without his baggage.

3. A community diviner should have no ego or pride about their divination job. Ideally, she should see herself as a vessel for the spirits or the Gods or fate or whatever, but no more than that. She should understand that having her gifts does not necessarily make her a more superior or less flawed human being than the other flawed humans who come seeking her advice, laying their flawed lives out on the table for her to see. She is a public service, and no more than that.

4. A community diviner should be constantly working toward better signal clarity, using whatever techniques he can find—meditation, grounding, stress-release, diet, herbs, drumming, whatever works. Signal clarity is crucial, for without it we are idiots talking to ourselves. He should be better than most people at putting aside at will any emotions and stressors that interfere with his signal clarity. At the same time, he should be experienced enough to know when those stressors have overwhelmed his signal with static, and be humble enough to step aside. See Rule 2.

5. A community diviner should be actively and constantly working toward being more self-aware and mindful, and shedding her psychological baggage. For us, every bag we carry is a possible monkey wrench in the signal clarity.

Self-awareness maintenance should be a full-time avocation for her. She should be more aware of her problems than most people, and have better control over them.

6. A community diviner should be painfully aware of the state of his mental health, and do whatever is necessary to make sure that any aberrations in the chemicals therein do not get in the way of the signal clarity. As a corollary, he should take concerned comments on his mental heath and the quality of his readings by people he trusts as issues to seriously consider, and not thrust them aside without due thought, discussion, and maybe getting a couple of readings on the subject. He should welcome such scrutiny from those he trusts and respects, because it's important outside perspective.

7. A community diviner should have some sort of regular spiritual path and/or discipline, and ideally some connection with Gods and/or spirits who help her interface with other Worlds and the information contained within. If her signal is good enough to get clean, clear information over the wire, it's good enough to get Someone on the phone to crosscheck with in ways that human beings can't.

8. A community diviner should take disbelief in his abilities in stride, and remember that no one is obligated to believe him. If he's right, it will all come out eventually; he should see the skepticism of other people as part of a healthy lack of gullibility and not take it personally. See Rule 3.

9. A community diviner should stand ready to help those who ask, but should not push her gifts aggressively on others whether they want it or not. Sometimes it means more to a person to figure something out themselves the hard way than to hear it come out of some random seer's mouth. If she is in doubt as to when to keep silent, she should get a reading from someone else on the subject.

10. A community diviner should make alliances with other diviners, and not just to have other people to refer folks to. He should make a practice of cross-checking dubious information with other diviners that he respects, preferably more than one at a time. The Gods don't mind if you want a second, third, and even fourth opinion—they'd rather you got the message right.

11. A community diviner should be grateful for the presence of other skilled diviners, seeing them as peers and colleagues rather than rivals. There's more than enough work to go around.

12. A community diviner should hold other community diviners to these standards, and aid them in achieving the same. If divination is to be considered a dependable source of otherworldly information—perhaps the most dependable source—then diviners need to be openly committed to reducing error by whatever margin they can. There will always be error, but honesty, self-awareness, humility, and hard work can significantly improve things. (Copyright by Raven Kaldera, 2008. Used with permission.)

I would add that, with the exception of consulting on a case with other colleagues (which is sometimes necessary), a community diviner should maintain the utmost levels of confidentiality and trust with his or her clients. Every diviner has to start somewhere, and Raven's guidelines are not a bad place to begin.

8 Magic

This chapter will explore the theory behind using the runes magically. I am not going to give a selection of rune charms or spells for the reader to "plug into" specific situations. I don't believe it works like that—or not very well, at any rate. Rune magic is too organic and individual a practice. Nor will I be providing a beginner's guide to "becoming a magician." There are several good and useful books in the resources section that can serve that purpose. Instead, I'm going to discuss what I believe to be the most important points in working with the runes for magic. I have found over the years that there is a protocol that ought to be followed when enlisting the aid and partnership of the runes; doing so can make the desired outcome that much more likely. Understanding the theory behind that protocol can make the whole process that much easier. This chapter will not teach you what to do as a magician; it will teach you to *be* a magician.

To quote my colleague Sophie Reicher, magic is "the craft of utilizing energy directly through the conduit of the will and body to effect circumstances in a clearly defined and predictable manner."[1] One can do this in a variety of ways, including directly, through raw manipulation of energy, through the use of specific props that help to focus the will, and through alliance with other spirits/beings (such as the runes). Working with the runes through galdr and in meditation will enhance one's sensitivity to natural energy, particularly to Wyrd and the power of the runes themselves. In order to work magic well, some degree of this sensitivity is necessary, either by training or via natural gift.

Before deciding to engage in any type of rune magic, I believe it is necessary to have a number of basics under one's proverbial belt. The rune magician ought to have thoroughly mastered grounding and centering, shielding, warding, and various cleansings, and ought to know how to protect, consecrate, and cleanse his or her working space. I highly recommend Reicher's book *Basic Psychic Hygiene* for a thorough examination of these practices. Mickaharic's *The Practice of Magic* and Regardie's *The One Year Manual* are also excellent places to begin. Each of these texts provides a series of graded exercises that, if practiced diligently, will provide the novice with an excellent foundation in safe magical practice. Before doing anything else, I urge the reader interested in magical practice to look into these resources.

It's amazing how effective magical practice often rests on common-sense care of the self. Any aspiring magician ought to have his or her emotional and psychological "house" in order. In other words, the would-be magician needs to be dealing with his or her issues first and foremost. As occultists have known for generations, the practice of magic can put one in touch with the shadow—the unexamined, repressed, and often unacknowledged aspects of our lives that we go out of our way to avoid. It's important to deal with any unresolved issues, fixations, or anxieties before starting to practice an occult art; otherwise, such practice can result in instability and neurosis. Magic should make one's life better. It should make the magician more effective. If it's not doing that, the magician needs to step back and take a clear and objective look as to why.

I'm sure that every occultist reading this has encountered the self-proclaimed magician endlessly bragging about his or her skill in the art, about his or her power, about his or her greatness—all while living in the basement of his or her parent's house, jobless, penniless, and with untreated mental or physical illness and a plethora of miscellaneous ailments. Something is clearly wrong with this picture. This is not the result of effective magical practice. We all go through periods when things may not be working out the way we had hoped, when illness threatens, when we grow depressed or suffer financial setbacks. That's part of living. But it shouldn't be a habit. It becomes cause for concern when, rather than seeing a period of personal setbacks, one sees a habit of crisis after crisis, drama after drama, *ad nauseum*. Magic should enhance one's life. If it doesn't, something is amiss.

So before even thinking about mucking around with Wyrd in this way, commit to eating healthily, getting therapy if you need it, getting your finances in order, and learning to honor your physical existence. Practicing magic is a wonderful thing. It's an energizing, fascinating, thrilling experience. But it is not a substitute for a well-lived life. The healthier and more well-balanced a person is, the safer and, by extension, more effective he or she will be when actively working magic. Being grounded is partly about learning the mental and energetic exercises needed to properly shunt internal energy where it needs to go. Externally, it's a matter of having your life in order as much as possible (and recognizing that this is an ongoing process just as learning is). The famous occult maxim, "As above, so below," applies beautifully here: What you do internally and energetically should reflect in your mundane, temporal, physical world, and vice versa. There's also the fact that the rune-spirits will latch onto any weakness and feed on it if you let them. That's something best avoided at all costs. You must be in control of the work you do, and that starts with being in control of yourself.

Ultimately, anything you do to get your life in order will benefit you esoterically. This includes getting out of debt. That may sound incredibly prosaic, but magic is not a solution for poor lifestyle management. Magic is about discipline, and, believe me, to work effectively in partnership with the runes in this way involves immense focus and discipline. That starts by disciplining the will. This includes learning to apply those principles to that most prosaic of places: the pocketbook. Basically, before even thinking about studying magic, get healthy, get solvent, and get sane, and do whatever you need to do (within reason) to stay that way. Magic has its own siren song, especially when the runes are involved, and if one isn't well-grounded in mundane life it's easy to get swept away.

So learn the basic exercises, get your mundane life in order, and study the runes. Establish a connection to them through the exercises and meditations provided in this book, and in any others that you discover. I would not suggest beginning your exploration of the runes with magical practice. I spent years working with them in both meditation and divination before I began to use them magically—and I was already a practicing occultist when I first encountered them. Getting one's life in a reasonable state of functionality may take months or even years. That's okay. There's no rush to learning magic. It's a lifetime endeavor. Better to take one's time and build a solid foundation from the very beginning.

After taking these necessary steps, the neophyte is ready to address the next truism about the occult: Magic is about the acquisition of power. This, too, has very clear-cut mundane applications. Our behavior can position us well or poorly with regard to this process of hunting for power. For example, every time you break your word, in no matter how small a matter, you sacrifice some measure of personal power and luck. Luck is part of the soul-matrix in Norse cosmology. Like Wyrd, we can inherit it from our Ancestors and affect it by our own choices. Even the best luck can be exhausted if it is squandered by foolish behavior. Luck is what puts us in the right place at the right time; it's one of the factors that helps insure that we don't get swept away in our quest for knowledge and occult power. A sensible magician learns to govern his or her actions wisely and well, even in the little things, such as whether or not you return a book borrowed from a friend the day you said you would, or whether or not you 'fess up when the cashier at the local coffee shop gives you too much change.

There are times in one's life as a magician when one needs to go into very gray moral areas, stretch one's luck to the utmost, and behave in ways that are not particularly nice (remember what I said earlier about "lawful" not always equaling "good"?). I prefer to bank both power and luck for those times instead of squandering it in a moment's lazy self-indulgence. Everyone who embarks on serious magical practice has to decide these things for him- or herself. I have found that the more I progress magically, the more obligations and debts (Wyrd-wise or to specific spirits or Beings) I incur. Sometimes it is a very delicate balancing act. No matter how carefully you govern your behavior, in Norse magic, there are no free rides. Ultimately there's always a price. The moment you think you don't have to pay a price, well, that thought, that surety, will put the collection process in motion. Everything affects our Wyrd. How much we pay, is a matter of degree and lawfulness; we rarely get to determine the price. I've just found it best not to help things veer down negative roads by my stupidity. It makes no sense to be collecting skill and power through the proverbial front door while squandering it and leaking it out the back. Understand that the effective practice of magic and the initiation into this art is a lifetime commitment. It affects everything, no matter how small, and it will change the way a practitioner views everything in his or her life. I will say right up front that one can be a very gifted diviner and rune-worker without ever practicing magic. Some people feel it's best to leave well enough alone. This is absolutely a valid option. There is no need to feel that one's relationship with the runes is not complete without engaging with this aspect of their power.

Magic isn't just about power, however; it's also about will and honing one's will. It is for this reason that so many books about magic focus on strengthening one's powers of concentration: energy follows desire, desire follows imagination, imagination follows thought, and thought follows will, and it is through the will that one's desires can be made manifest. Will isn't strengthened only by daily meditation and contemplation; it is strengthened by consciously endeavoring to develop useful habits every day throughout our lives. Every day, whether one is actively engaged in magic or not, can becoming a training ground that can prepare the neophyte for esoteric work while helping him or her to remain properly grounded in the mundane world, which where we want the effects of our magic to manifest after all. As above, so below.

Now I would like to touch on an aspect of practice that many new rune magicians might find distasteful or even frightening: the use of one's own blood as a magical tool. For those who seriously work with runes, particularly in magic, sooner or later the question of whether or not to do this will come up. I've always found the runes to be more than a bit hungry for life energy. Blood truly is the essence of life, our connection to our Ancestors, and the genetic map of all we are and everything we have come from. Because of this, the drawing of blood is a sacred threshold. The magic of this sacrifice lies as much in the will that makes the offering as the offering itself. To feed the runes, it must be drawn with clear and careful intent. It must be living blood. (By the way, menstrual blood is not an acceptable offering because it is, in effect, waste blood, something the body would get rid of anyway. Menstruation is a time of cleansing, of purifying the body, not of collecting and honing that internal power. It is not the blood of life, but rather the blood that would have nourished life. Menstrual blood has some uses in magic, but this is not one of them.)

This is not a topic that most of us are willing to talk openly about, but I must write from my own experience of working the runes, and that experience has led me to conclude that, eventually, the giving of blood is inevitable. I want to be very clear here: I am talking about giving one's own blood in a controlled and safe manner. Period. There are ways to do this safely and sanely. Earlier in this book, I talked about using diabetic lancets to draw blood, which is actually one of the easiest and most effective methods. With this method, one does not run the risk of causing potentially fatal damage, as one would with a knife. I keep diabetic lancets and alcohol swabs in my diviner's kit right along with my runes. I use the swabs to wipe down my finger before using the lancet and again to clean the very small puncture afterwards. (I've never gotten any infection from using lancets, but better safe than sorry.) Lancets should be used only once. Never share them and never reuse them. They should be disposed of properly in a "sharps" container that is clearly marked as containing bio-hazardous materials. These containers can be purchased at any pharmacy.

There is more to using blood esoterically than simply knowing how to follow sterile procedures, however. A large part of working with blood means examining how you feel about it. Any unresolved motivations in magic, any unexamined issues, any unacknowledged fears can negatively affect the magic you're trying to cast, unraveling it and rendering it ineffective. Blood is a powerful substance, and the use of blood a highly charged act in our culture, and rightly so. Blood can mean many things, including:

>> Power. It is the raw life essence. By feeding the runes with one's own blood, it is possible to create a powerful connection.

>> Memory. Blood contains a map of our entire ancestry. For this reason, blood can be used magically to mark something as undeniably yours. (Of course, in many magical systems, blood is such a powerful link that one can be tracked via the esoteric connection forged by one's blood. This is why systems of magic such Hoodoo emphasize extreme caution when dealing with blood, hair, body fluids, nail parings, and so on.)

>> Sacrifice. Blood has been associated with religious sacrifice in nearly every religion throughout history.

>> Eroticism. For some, the spilling of one's own blood for someone or for a higher purpose has strong overtones of eroticism. This is okay, as the runes can feed on sexual energies, too. It's just another kind of energy after all.

Blood is both life and death, taboo and sacred. It is at the same time both terribly dangerous and terribly sacred. These can be difficult and disturbing concepts for modern people. Our fear of blood for health reasons parallels the ancient fear of blood for magical and religious reasons. In both cases, blood carries with it a fear of contamination. Perhaps one of the reasons that blood has always been a common sacrificial offering is that the process of making this offering safely highlights the fact that inconvenience is not sacrifice. To do this work well, the rune-worker must know the difference between a gift, an offering, and a sacrifice. Sometimes the lines between these things are fine and blurry. The question facing every rune-worker who chooses to feed the runes in this manner is this: How can we make blood sacred again when our entire cultural approach to blood has been affected by the fear of disease (and rightly so)?

Giving blood is all about establishing a working relationship through the politics of exchange. It's about using a gift (one's own blood) to establish hierarchy and to negotiate power exchange. Essentially, the act of giving a gift requires some form of payment in return, which in and of itself commits the giver and receiver to an endless cycle of reciprocity.[2] This is absolutely true with the runes, as well. The giving and receiving of a gift can be a terrifying and dangerous thing, fraught not only with social obligations but with spiritual ones, as well. This is aptly illustrated in the Havamal, where the God Odin states: "Betra er óbeðit en sé ofblótit, ey sér til gildis gjöf; betra er ósent en sé ofsóit." ("'Tis better not to pray than too much offer; a gift ever looks to a return. 'Tis better not to send than too much consume.")[3]

That which is sacred is invested with a quality of contagion, allowing it to infiltrate the world of the profane unless carefully bounded by taboo and necessary precautions.[4] Any breech of these carefully defined boundaries may cause fear, ambivalence, and/or outright hostility. Many rituals involving sacrifice are approached with a tension approaching outright fear of exactly that: that the world of the profane will be contaminated by that which is sacred.[5] Often, the threshold marking the doorway between the sacred and profane is marked through the giving of blood. Regardless of what you end up giving the runes, remember that you're establishing and maintaining a relationship based on reciprocity and gift-giving. That exchange is the core of the relationship and it must be an ongoing process. This is true in divination and even more so in magic.

Another point that must be touched upon is that of courtesy. This can be summed up in one sentence: Clean up your mess (or better yet, try not to make one in the first place). There are several facets to doing this.

Firstly, respect the runes; they are your allies. Don't break your word to them. Maintain a reasonably frequent exchange of gifts. Don't call upon them for inconsequential things that you could accomplish by patience, common sense, or good old-fashioned hard work. A colleague once told me a true story of a one of his clients. This woman was a very skilled diviner. She became so obsessed that she began to use it all the time to answer the most innocuous of questions. Eventually it got so bad that she would whip out her divination tools to decide between chicken and fish at a restaurant. That was when Wyrd, the fates, the Gods, or her Ancestors—I'm not sure who—took away her gift for divination, and rightly so. Do not be this woman. The runes do not care about your lost bracelet, your choice of a main course at dinner, whether you should date person X or person Y, or any other quotidian minutiae of life. Instead, reserve the use of runes for reading or affecting Wyrd, for changing your luck, and for creating or blocking specific opportunities. Use them in healing and protecting and in helping to create the type of life you want to live. Don't abuse their aid by wasting or disregarding it. They will only tolerate this for so long.

Secondly, dispose of any materials properly. This means using a sharps container for lancets. Don't leave bloody tissues, alcohol swabs, or any other accoutrements of your practice lying around. Keep your tools in good working order at all times.

Finally, try not to be stupid or sloppy. Be measured in your use of magic. As someone who has gotten called in as the magical equivalent of a hazmat team to clean up after novice magicians more than once, I beg you: please be measured in what you attempt. Learn how to protect yourself and your space. Learn how to cleanse it after your workings. The secrets of the universe and all the power the runes hold are not going to be available to you in just a few short, easy lessons, if ever! The runes will test each magician over and over again, parceling out their wisdom based on what the magician earns. Please try not overestimate your skill.

Ultimately it comes down to this: If you believe that magic works, you have to take responsibility for the fact that it works. Treat learning and practicing and caring for your surroundings and tools the same way you would approach learning to shoot a gun, because on an esoteric level, magic can be just as dangerous.

Suggested Reading

Books on Runes

Aswynn, Freya. *Northern Mysteries and Magic*. St. Paul, Minn.: Llewellyn Publications, 2002.

———. *Principles of Runes*. Hammersmith, UK: Thorsons Publishers, 2000.

Page, R.I. *An Introduction to English Runes*. Suffolk, UK: Boydell Press, 1999.

Paxson, Diana. *Taking up the Runes*. York Beach, Maine: Red Wheel/Weiser Books, 2005.

Peterson, James. *The Enchanted Alphabet*. Wellingborough, UK: Aquarian Press, 1988.

Pollington, Stephen. *Rudiments of Runelore*. Norfolk, UK: Anglo-Saxon Books, 1995.

Thorsson, Edred. *Futhark*. York Beach, Maine: Samuel Weiser, Inc., 1984.

———. *Northern Magic Rune Mysteries and Shamanism*. St. Paul, Minn.: Llewellyn Publications, 2003.

———. *Runecaster's Handbook: The Well of Wyrd*. York Beach, Maine: Samuel Weiser, Inc., 1999.

————. *Runelore*. York Beach, Maine: Samuel Weiser, Inc., 1987.

Books on Norse Cosmology and Religion

Bauschatz, Paul. *The Well and the Tree*. Boston, Mass.: University of Massachusetts Press, 1982.

Crossley-Holland, Kevin. *Norse Myths*. New York, N.Y.: Pantheon Books, 1980.

Ellis-Davidson, H.R. *Gods and Myths of Northern Europe*. New York, N.Y.: Penguin Books, 1990.

————. *The Road to Hel*. Westport, Conn.: Greenwood Press, 1968.

Filan, Kenaz and Raven Kaldera. *Drawing Down the Spirits*. Rochester, Vt.: Destiny Books, 2009.

Kershaw, Kris. Odin the One-Eyed God. Washington, D.C.: Journal of Indo-European Studies Monograph Number 36, 2000.

Krasskova, Galina. *Exploring the Northern Tradition*. Franklin Lakes, N.J.: New Page Books, 2005.

Krasskova, Galina and Raven Kaldera. *Northern Tradition for the Solitary Practitioner*. Franklin Lakes, N.J.: New Page Books, 2009.

Paxson, Diana. *Essential Asatru*. New York, N.Y.: Citadel Books, 2006.

Poetic Edda. Translation by Lee Hollander. Austin, Tex.: University of Texas Press, 1962.

Prose Edda. Translation by Jesse L Byock. London: Penguin Books, 2005.

Simek, Rudolf. *The Dictionary of Northern Mythology*. Stuttgart: Alfred Kröner Verlag, 1993.

Turville-Petre, E.O.G. *Myth and Religion of the North*. New York, NY: Holt, Rinehart and Winston, 1964.

Children's Books on Norse Cosmology

D'Aulaire, Edgar and Ingri D'Aulaire. *Norse Gods and Giants*. New York, N.Y.: The New York Review of Books, 2005.

Green, Roger Lancelyn. *Myths of the Norsemen*. New York, N.Y.: Puffin Classics, 1994.

Books on Northern Tradition Shamanism

Eliade, Mircea. *Shamanism: Archaic Techniques of Ecstasy*. Princeton, N.J.: Princeton University Press, 1964.

Filan, Kenaz and Raven Kaldera. *Drawing Down the Spirits*. Rochester, Vt: Destiny Books, 2009.

Kaldera, Raven. *Jotunbok: Working With the Giants of the Northern Tradition*. Hubbardson, Mass.: Asphodel Press, 2006.

———. *Pathwalker's Guide to the Nine Worlds*. Hubbardston, Mass.: Asphodel Press, 2006.

———. *Wyrdwalkers: Techniques of Northern Tradition Shamanism*. Hubbardston, Mass.: Asphodel Press, 2007.

———. *Wightridden: Paths of Northern Tradition Shamanism*. Hubbardston, Mass.: Asphodel Press, 2007.

Price, Neil. *The Viking Way*. Oxford, UK: Oxbow Books, 2008.

Books on Magic, Energy-Work, Cleansings, and Hoodoo

Fortune, Dion. *Psychic Self Defense*. San Francisco, Calif.: Red Wheel/Weiser Books, 2001.

Denning and Phillips. *The Practical Guide to Psychic Self Defense*. St. Paul, Minn.: Llewellyn Publications, 1983.

Mauss, Marcel. *A General Theory of Magic*. London, UK: Routledge Classics, 2001.

Mickaharic, Draja. *Magic Simplified*. Bloomington, IN: Xlibris Books, 2002.

———. *The Practice of Magic*. York Beach, Maine: Red Wheel/Weiser, 2006.

———. *Spiritual Cleansing*. York Beach, Maine: Red Wheel/Weiser, 2003.

Reicher, Sophie. *Basic Psychic Hygiene*. Hubbardston, Mass.: Ellhorn Books, 2008.

Yronwode, Catherine. *Hoodoo Herb and Root Magic*. Forrestville, Calif.: Luckymojo Books, 2002.

Miscellaneous Texts

Asad, Talal. *Formations of the Secular*. Stanford, Calif.: Stanford University Press, 2003.

Beidelman, T.O. "Agonistic Exchange: Homeric Reciprocity and the Heritage of Simmel and Mauss." *Cultural Anthropology*, Vol. 4, No. 3 (Aug. 1989), pp. 227–259. Accessed June 24, 2009 at: *http://www.jstor.org/stable/656460*.

Frazer, James. *The Golden Bough*. Oxford, UK: Oxford University Press, 1998.

Glucklich, Ariel. *Sacred Pain*. New York, N.Y.: Oxford University Press, 2001.

Godelier, Maurice. *The Enigma of the Gift*. Chicago, Ill.: Polity Press, 1999.

Mauss, Marcel. *The Gift: The Form and Reason of Exchange in Archaic Societies*. London, UK: Routledge Press, 1990.

Websites

The God's Mouths: *http://godsmouths.blogspot.com*.

Northern Tradition Shamanism: *http://www.northernshamanism.org*.

Lucky Mojo correspondence course in Hoodoo: *http://www.luckymojo.com*.

Bibliography

Aswynn, Freya. Northern Mysteries and Magic. St. Paul, Minn.: Llewellyn Publications, 2002.

———. Principles of Runes. Hammersmith, UK: Thorsons Publishers, 2000.

Bauschatz, Paul. The Well and the Tree. Boston, Mass: University of Massachusetts Press, 1982.

Beidelman, T.O. "Agonistic Exchange: Homeric Reciprocity and the Heritage of Simmel and Mauss." Source: *Cultural Anthropology*, Vol. 4, No. 3 (Aug. 1989), pp. 227–259. Accessed June 24, 2009 at: *http://www.jstor.org/stable/656460*.

Crossley-Holland, Kevin. *Norse Myths*. New York, N.Y.: Pantheon Books, 1980.

Denning and Phillips. *The Practical Guide to Psychic Self Defense*. St. Paul, Minn.: Llewellyn Publications, 1983.

Eliade, Mircea. *Shamanism: Archaic Techniques of Ecstasy*. Princeton, N.J.: Princeton University Press, 1964.

Ellis-Davidson, H.R. *Gods and Myths of Northern Europe*. New York, N.Y.: Penguin Books, 1990.

————. *The Road to Hel*. Westport, Conn.: Greenwood Press, 1968.

Filan, Kenaz and Kaldera, Raven. *Drawing Down the Spirits*. Rochester, Vt: Destiny Books, 2009.

Fortune, Dion. *Psychic Self Defense*. San Francisco, Calif.: Red Wheel/Weiser Books, 2001.

Godelier, Maurice. *The Enigma of the Gift*. Chicago, Ill.: Polity Press, 1999.

Kaldera, Raven. *Jotunbok: Working with the Giants of the Northern Tradition*. Hubbardson, Mass.: Asphodel Press, 2006.

————. *Pathwalker's Guide to the Nine Worlds*. Hubbardston, Mass.: Asphodel Press, 2006.

————. *Wyrdwalkers: Techniques of Northern Tradition Shamanism*. Hubbardston, Mass.: Asphodel Press, 2007.

————. *Wightridden: Paths of Northern Tradition Shamanism*. Hubbardston, Mass.: Asphodel Press, 2007.

Krasskova, Galina. *Exploring the Northern Tradition*. Franklin Lakes, N.J.: New Page Books, 2005.

Krasskova, Galina and Raven Kaldera. *Northern Tradition for the Solitary Practitioner*. Franklin Lakes, N.J.: New Page Books, 2009.

Mauss, Marcel. *The Gift: The Form and Reason of Exchange in Archaic Societies*. London, UK: Routledge Press, 1990.

Mickaharic, Draja. *Magic Simplified*. Bloomington, Ind.: Xlibris Books, 2002.

————. *The Practice of Magic*. York Beach, Maine: Red Wheel/Weiser, 2006.

————. *Spiritual Cleansing*. York Beach, Maine: Red Wheel/Weiser, 2003.

Page, R.I. *An Introduction to English Runes*. Suffolk, UK: Boydell Press, 1999.

Paxson, Diana. *Essential Asatru*. New York, N.Y.: Citadel Books, 2006.

———. *Taking up the Runes*. York Beach, Maine: Red Wheel/Weiser Books, 2005.

Peterson, James. *The Enchanted Alphabet*. Wellingborough, UK: Aquarian Press, 1988.

Poetic Edda. Translation by Lee Hollander. Austin, Tex.: University of Texas Press, 1962.

Pollington, Stephen. *Rudiments of Runelore*. Norfolk: UK: Anglo-Saxon Books, 1995.

Price, Neil. *The Viking Way*. Oxford, UK: Oxbow Books, 2008.

Prose Edda. Translation by Jesse L Byock. London: Penguin Books, 2005.

Reicher, Sophie. *Basic Psychic Hygiene*. Hubbardston, Mass.: Ellhorn Books, 2008.

Thorsson, Edred. *Futhark*. York Beach, Maine: Samuel Weiser, Inc., 1984.

———. *Northern Magic Rune Mysteries and Shamanism*. St. Paul, Minn.: Llewellyn Publications, 2003.

———. *Runecaster's Handbook: The Well of Wyrd*. York Beach, Maine: Samuel Weiser, Inc., 1999.

———. *Runelore*. York Beach, Maine: Samuel Weiser, Inc., 1987.

Turville-Petre. *E.O.G. Myth and Religion of the North*. New York, N.Y.: Holt, Rinehart and Winston, 1964.

Yronwode, Catherine. *Hoodoo Herb and Root Magic*. Forrestville, Calif.: Luckymojo Books, 2002.

*C*hapter Notes

Chapter 1

1. Odin has more than 100 by-names, or *heiti*, listed in the surviving lore.

2. From *http://www.cauldronfarm.com/writing/eightfold.html*.

3. So much so that one modern ordeal worker, Anya Kless, a devotee of Odin, refers to Him by the names "Thirsty for Pain" and "Hungry for Flesh." She is not alone in these attributions within the Northern Tradition community. Similar comments from devotees of Odin can frequently be heard, particularly those who also identify themselves as ordeal workers. This is not to say that every single rune-worker or devotee of Odin must be an ordeal worker. Nothing could be further from the truth. Odin has many paths. In addition to being a God of the ordeal, He is also a God of wisdom, passion, healing, kingship, and a thousand other things. Also, devotion is a very individual thing. Although ordeal may lie at the heart of His own sacrifice and winning of the runes, it does not follow that every single rune-worker must also embrace ordeal. Odin is about much more than *just* ordeal. He (and the runes to

some extent) will point each person in the direction of the work to which he or she is best suited. That said, my own work with the runes and my own devotion to Odin led me to ordeal work, and it is through that lens that I approach this craft. I write primarily on His ordeal on Yggdrasil here because it is integral to working with the runes: it is *the* story of how they came to be accessible to us.

4. Eliade, p. 69–70.
5. *Poetic Edda,* Bellows translation, p. 60.
6. Simek, p. 272. See also *Poetic Edda*, Havamal stanza 144.
7. Simek, p. 272.
8. Kaldera, p. 39.
9. Ibid.
10. Quoted from a currently unpublished paper titled *Ordeal Work, Body Modification, and the Use of Pain in Northern Tradition Paganism,* first presented at "Religion Matters," an academic conference hosted by Ohio State University on October 4, 2008.
11. Frazer, p. 405.
12. Glucklich, p. 115.
13. Glucklich, p. 144–47.
14. From an unpublished article titled "Sacrifice, Odin and the Ritual of Blót in Modern Norse Paganism" by Galina Krasskova.
15. Turville-Petre, p. 48.
16. *The Dream of the Rood*, accessed March 22, 2009 from *http://faculty.uca.edu/jona/texts/rood.htm*.
17. From an unpublished article titled "Sacrifice, Odin and the Ritual of Blót in Modern Norse Paganism" by Galina Krasskova.
18. Frazer, p. 11.

19. From an unpublished article titled "Sacrifice, Odin and the Ritual of Blót in Modern Norse Paganism" by Galina Krasskova.

20. Asad, p. 69.

21. Asad, p. 71.

22. Asad, p. 79.

23. From an unpublished paper titled "Ordeal Work, Body Modification, and the Use of Pain in Northern Tradition Paganism" first presented at the Religion Matters academic conference, Ohio State University, October 4, 2008.

24. Ibid.

25. Kershaw, p. 3.

26. Kershaw notes that this specifically indicates that Odin has the power to blind armies with terror during battle. But given that Odin is traditionally known as a God of warriors, it seems to me that it could just as easily be translated as one who blinds his armies *to* terror.

27. From an unpublished article titled "Sacrifice, Odin and the Ritual of Blót in Modern Norse Paganism" by Galina Krasskova.

28. Turville-Petre, p. 47.

29. *Seven Viking Romances* (trans. Magnusson, Magnus and Hermann Palsson).

30. Frazer, p. 324.

Chapter 3

1. Paxson, p. 175.

2. Larrington, p. 34.

3. Larrington, p. 35. I have seen some translations substitute "worship" for "sacrifice," and "sacrifice" for "slaughter."

The idea of slaughter/sacrifice refers to ritual sacrifice of an animal, that is, the ritual of blót.

4. Simek, p. 272.

5. From *www.quotes.net/quote/4555*. Accessed October, 2009.

6. All translations of the rune poems are quoted with permission from *http://www.ragweedforge.com/poems.html*.

7. Modern rune poems have no basis in lore. However, writing rune poems is an excellent way to connect with the runes themselves. I include Vongvisith's poems here as an example of how one might choose to interact with the runes.

8. *Poetic Edda*, Havamal stanza 145.

9. For more information on the cultural relevance of gift-giving, I recommend *The Gift: the Form and Reason of Exchange in Archaic Societies* by Marcel Mauss, and *The Enigma of the Gift*. By Maurice Godelier. I also recommend an article by T.O Beidelman titled "Agonistic Exchange: Homeric Reciprocity and the Heritage of Simmel and Mauss" in Cultural Anthropology magazine, Vol. 4, No. 3 (Aug., 1989), pp. 227–259.

10. Some scholars believe that Christ here is a substitution for one of Odin's by-names, a later Christianization of the poem.

11. Many rune-workers believe that the word "God" here originally indicated Frey.

12. Frothi is a by-name of Frey.

13. Ecclesiastes 3:1–8

14. Paxson, p. 139.

15. From the Second Merseburger Charm, accessed June 24, 2009, at *http://www.hs-augsburg.de/~harsch/germanica/Chronologie/08Jh/Merseburg/mer_text.html#02*.

16. Additional translation of this stanza from *http://www. northvegr.org/lore/runes/002.php*, accessed June 24, 2009.

17. Pollington, p. 24.

18. *The Prophet*, from *http://www.katsandogz.com/onmarriage. html* accessed June 24, 2009.

19. Pollington, p. 25.

Chapter 4

1. Pollington, p. 29.

2. Krasskova, *Walking Toward Yggdrasil*, p. 23.

Chapter 5

1. From personal correspondence with the author.

2. Perhaps because She determines the time of one's death, Skuld is sometimes also numbered amongst the Valkyrie, Odin's warrior-women who ride into battle, selecting the best warriors for the honor of Valhalla.

3. Krasskova, p. 121.

4. Just as there are ways to access a person's Wyrd, there are an equal number of ways for a person to protect his or her Wyrd from being accessed. It takes no small skill in magic to do this effectively, though. The easiest method that I can describe is to center oneself and slip into what I call "Wyrd-sight"—the state of mind wherein one can see or otherwise sense the patterns of Wyrd. Locate your own strand (and you will know it when you see it, as it will flow from you), then galdr and cast runes of protection in an extended perimeter along and around the strands. Algiz is an excellent rune to use for this. Or, when you shield yourself energetically, visualize those shields also extending along your personal threads.

Chapter 6
1. Sophie Reicher, *Basic Psychic Hygiene* (quoted with permission).
2. Ibid.

Chapter 7
1. Tacitus, p. 145–146.
2. Ibid., p. 143.
3. Depending on whether they restrict themselves to the Elder Futhark or incorporate the Anglo-Saxon or Northumbrian Futhorc, some people like to select 24 or 33 sticks and throw them down, reading from whatever runes are created by the crossing tines. I haven't seen this very often, but it is a valid method of reading.
4. From personal correspondence with the author.

Chapter 8
1. Reicher, p. 93.
2. Mauss, p. ix.
3. *Poetic Edda*, Thorpe translation. This paragraph was excerpted from an unpublished article titled "Sacrifice, Odin and the Ritual of Blót in Modern Norse Paganism" by Galina Krasskova.
4. Durkheim, p. 236–237.
5. From an unpublished article titled "Sacrifice, Odin and the Ritual of Blót in Modern Norse Paganism" by Galina Krasskova.

# Index

About the Author

GALINA KRASSKOVA has been a Heathen priest and devotee of Odin for close to 20 years. She is a member of Urdabrunnr Kindred in New York, Ironwood Kindred in Massachusetts, Asatru in Frankfurt, Germany, and the First Kingdom Church of Asphodel in Massachusetts. She has written numerous books on the Northern Tradition, including *Exploring the Northern Tradition*, *The Whisperings of Woden*, *Full Fathom Five*, and *Northern Tradition for the Solitary Practitioner* (with Raven Kaldera). She holds a diploma in interfaith ministry, and a BA and an MA in religious studies. She currently works for the Interfaith Fellowship in New York City and is in the process of pursuing her PhD.